Chowders, Bisques and Soups

Recipes from Canada's Best Chefs

Elaine Elliot and Virginia Lee

Formac Publishing Company Limited
Halifax

Formac Publishing Company Limited acknowledges the support of the Cultural Affairs Section, Nova Scotia Department of Tourism and Culture. We acknowledge the financial support of the Government of Canada through the Book Publishing Industry Development Program (BPIDP) for our publishing activities.

We acknowledge the support of the Canada Council for the Arts for our publishing program.

National Library of Canada Cataloguing in Publication Data

Elliot, Elaine, 1939-
    Chowders, bisques & soups : recipes from Canada's best chefs / Elaine Elliot & Virginia Lee.

includes index.

ISBN 0-88780-649-X

    1. Soups. I. Lee, Virginia, 1947- II. Title.
III. Title: Chowders, bisques and soups.

TX757.E45 2004   641.8'13   C2004-904429-X

Photo Credits

All photos by Janet Kimber except for the following:
Hamid Attie: 9, 54, 93
Dwayne Coon: 14, 38, 43, 90, 91
Terry Manzo: 11top right, 40, 42, 47, 52, 57, 58, 61, 66, 67, 70, 71
Formac Publishing Company Limited: 22, 44, 83, 85, 87, 89

Dedication

This book is dedicated to our parents Margaret and Frank who are always in our hearts.

Formac Publishing Company Limited
5502 Atlantic Street
Halifax, Nova Scotia
B3H 1G4
www.formac.ca

Printed and bound in Canada

Contents

Introduction

Take a peek inside any good restaurant's kitchen and you will find a simmering pot of soup. The aroma, texture and balance of flavours has been perfected by the chef. Now you can indulge in these professional secrets by preparing these chunky chowders, smooth bisques and hearty soups — recipes collected from chefs across Canada.

There seems to be no end to the diversity of soups and the chefs' recipes emphasize fresh ingredients used in innovative ways. They also showcase regional specialties. Atlantic Canada's chefs shared soups filled with haddock, clams, salmon and scallops, while British Columbia chefs contributed chowders featuring oysters, mussels and swimming scallops. Meanwhile from Manitoba, we were sent a Chicken and Corn Chowder and from Ontario, Pepper Pot Chowder.

For elegant dining, there is nothing so smooth as a delicately flavoured bisque, such as Chestnut Bisque or Lobster Bisque Cappuccino. To beat the heat, chilled soup could be the first item on your menu. For tradition with a new twist, turn to the Chilled Vichyssoise with Smoked Salmon and Dill or Summer Gazpacho with Roasted Corn and Crab Salsa. Summer and fruit go together in recipes such as Raspberry Soup and Blueberry Soup. If you enjoy a fusion of international ingredients you will want to try Posole Soup with its Mexican roots or the delicate Thai Sweet Potato and Coconut Bisque.

No elaborate cooking equipment is

required. A large, heavy-bottomed saucepan is essential along with utensils for preparing vegetables, fruit, meat and fish. Either a food processor, or a blender or hand-held blender is sufficient for pureeing bisques and cream soups.

This book has been a labour of love and we thank our culinary friends, the professional chefs from across Canada, for generously sharing with us their recipes.

— EE and VL

"I live on good soups, not fine words."

— Molière

Curried Potato & Leek Chowder with Sauteed Seafood Salad

Chowders

Being from the east coast, we are biased about chowder — are not all chowders made with fresh seafood and loads of cream? But our chef friends from across the country were eager to share their recipes made with ingredients indigenous to their respective areas.

For example, Chanterelle and Scallop Chowder from Kingfisher Ocean Restaurant in British Columbia features local "swimming scallops," a mollusk native to the waters surrounding Vancouver Island. Curried Potato and Salmon Chowder from Nova Scotia's Amherst Shore Country Inn features salmon, haddock, scallops and lobster, all from the Atlantic ocean. Fear not, when regional ingredients are not available, we offer substitutions.

WEST COAST CHOWDER

BISHOP'S RESTAURANT, VANCOUVER, BC

This chowder with its trio of shellfish and hint of aromatic herbs will, as restaurant owner John Bishop says, "Cure any rainy-day blues." We tested the recipe using tomato sauce to create a red chowder, but for a white chowder you can substitute the tomato sauce with equal amounts of heavy cream.

1 lb	clams in shell	500 g
1 lb	mussels in shell	500 g
1 cup	white wine, divided	250 mL
2 tbsp	butter	30 mL
1/2 cup	diced onion	125 mL
1/2 cup	diced carrot	125 mL
1/2 cup	diced celery	125 mL
1/2 cup	diced potato	125 mL
1/4 cup	diced bell pepper	50 mL
3/4 tsp	ground fennel seeds	3 mL
3/4 tsp	ground coriander seeds	3 mL
3/4 tsp	dried basil	3 mL
3/4 tsp	dried oregano	3 mL
2 tsp	gin, optional:	10 mL
	1/2 tsp (2 mL) juniper berries	
4 cups	tomato sauce (recipe follows)	1 L
5 cups	fish stock	1.25 L
12	oysters, shucked and chopped	12
6	slices bacon, chopped,	

(fried and drained on paper towels)

Rinse clams and mussels with cold water. Discard any that are cracked or do not open when lightly tapped. In a large saucepan, bring clams, mussels and 1/2 cup (125 mL) of the white wine to a boil; cook 5 to 8 minutes until the shellfish open. Discard any that do not open. Remove and reserve clam and mussel meat; strain and reserve cooking liquid.

Heat butter in a large stockpot over low heat. Add vegetables and herbs; cook until vegetables are softened, about 10 minutes. Raise heat to medium-high; add gin, remaining 1/2 cup (125 mL) white wine; deglaze pan, stirring constantly.

Add tomato sauce, fish stock and reserved shellfish liquid; bring to a boil. Reduce heat, cover and simmer 30 to 45 minutes. Add clams, mussels and oysters; return to serving temperature, and adjust seasoning.

Garnish with crispy chopped bacon.

Serves 6 to 8

TOMATO SAUCE

The chef at Bishop's Restaurant recommends that the tomatoes be as ripe as possible. "If you can put your finger through them, all the better."

3 tbsp	olive oil	45 mL
3	onions, peeled and chopped	
3 cups	canned whole Italian plum tomatoes	750 mL
4½ cups	diced fresh tomatoes, cored and seeded	1050 mL

Heat oil in a large saucepan over medium-low heat. Add onions; cover and cook until softened, about 10 minutes. Add tomatoes; simmer for 45 minutes to 1 hour, stirring frequently.

In a food processor, puree sauce. Store, refrigerated 5 days; do not freeze.

Makes 4 cups sauce

CURRIED POTATO AND SALMON CHOWDER

THE AMHERST SHORE COUNTRY INN,
LORNEVILLE, NS

The close proximity of the Northumberland Strait provides innkeeper Mary Laceby with an abundance of fresh seafood. She advises that dense fish, such as halibut or tuna, can replace the salmon in this recipe.

¼ cup	butter	50 mL
1 cup	finely chopped onions	250 mL
2 cups	potatoes, peeled and diced	500 mL
2 cups	chicken stock	500 mL
1½ tsp	curry powder	7 mL
2 cups	heavy cream (35% M.F.)	500 mL
4 oz	poached salmon, flaked	125 g

salt and freshly ground pepper to taste

Melt butter in a heavy saucepan; sauté onions until translucent. Stir in potatoes, chicken stock and curry powder; simmer until vegetables are tender, about 15 minutes. Stir in cream and simmer until slightly thickened.

Gently stir in flaked salmon and adjust seasoning with salt and freshly ground pepper.

Serves 4

PEPPER POT CHOWDER

THE WESTOVER INN, ST. MARYS, ONTARIO

The "zip" in this chowder comes from sambal oelek, an Indonesian condiment found in the international food section of the supermarket.

¾ cup	unsalted butter	175 mL
¾ cup	all-purpose flour	175 mL
3 tbsp	vegetable oil	45 mL
1	small white onion, finely diced	1
3	medium-sized peppers, (1 each-green, red, and yellow, cut in 1/4 inch (0.5 cm) pieces)	3
1 tbsp	minced garlic	15 mL
1 tbsp	white wine	15 mL
6 cups	chicken stock	1.5 L
¾ tsp	sambal oelek* (see page 17)	3 mL
¾ tsp	Worcestershire sauce	3 mL
½ tsp	salt	2 mL
¼ tsp	freshly ground pepper	1 mL
3 cups	milk	750 mL

Melt butter in a small saucepan and whisk in flour, forming a roux. Cook, stirring constantly until golden brown in colour, about 2 minutes. Remove from heat and reserve.

Heat oil in a large skillet over medium-high heat. Sauté onions, stir constantly for 1 minute. Add peppers and garlic; sauté an additional 2 minutes. Deglaze pan with white wine. Stir in 2 cups (500 mL) of the chicken stock, sambal oelek, Worcestershire sauce, salt and pepper; simmer for 5 minutes.

In a large saucepan, bring milk and remaining chicken stock to a boil; reduce to a simmer and whisk in reserved roux. Continue to cook until slightly thickened; stir in vegetable mixture and simmer for 10 minutes. If desired, adjust seasoning with salt and pepper.

Serves 6 to 8

CURRIED POTATO & LEEK CHOWDER WITH SAUTEED SEAFOOD SALAD

CHIVES CANADIAN BISTRO, HALIFAX, NS

Chef Darren Lewis suggests using your own favourite curry powder as it will always be the "best".

This chowder has great eye appeal and at Chives Canadian Bistro, the sautéed seafood salad is served in a crispy "potato collar"; however, the chef says that hollowed-out puff pastry shells are also a delicious way to serve the Seafood Salad.

3 tbsp	unsalted butter	45 mL
4	large leeks, white part only, (cleaned and chopped)	4
2	cloves garlic, minced	2
1-1½ tbsp	curry powder, or to taste	15-22 mL
½ cup	white wine	125 mL
3 cups	chicken stock, (optional: seafood or vegetable stock)	750 mL
1	large Yukon gold potato, (peeled and thinly sliced)	1
½ cup	heavy cream (35% M.F.)	125 mL
1 cup	potato, finely diced, (cooked and cooled)	250 mL
½ cup	carrot, finely diced, (cooked and cooled)	125 mL
6	puff pastry shells, baked	6

Sautéed Seafood Salad (recipe follows)
fresh chopped cilantro for garnish
chili oil for garnish

Melt butter in a large saucepan over medium heat. Sauté leek and garlic; stir frequently, until softened and beginning to brown, about 6 to 8 minutes. Add curry powder and stir constantly; cook until fragrant, about 1 minute. Deglaze pan with wine and reduce slightly.

Add chicken stock and potatoes; bring to a boil. Lower heat to simmer, cover and cook 20 to 25 minutes, until potatoes are soft.

In a blender, puree soup in batches until smooth and creamy. If necessary, pass through a fine sieve. Return soup to saucepan; add cream and adjust consistency with additional stock if needed. Add diced potato and carrot; bring to serving temperature.

Place a warm puff pastry shell in the centre of each soup bowl. Fill pastry with seafood salad and ladle chowder around it. Garnish with fresh cilantro and a drizzle of chili oil.

Serves 6

SAUTEED SEAFOOD SALAD

1 tbsp	unsalted butter	15 mL
1 tbsp	chopped shallot	15 mL
1	garlic clove, minced	1
12	raw medium-sized shrimp, (31/35 count)	12
12	medium sea scallops	12
6	cooked lobster claws, shelled	6
1 tbsp	chopped cilantro	15 mL
1 tbsp	chopped chives	15 mL
1½ tbsp	lemon juice	22 mL
salt and pepper to taste		

Melt butter in a small skillet. Sauté shallots and garlic until lightly browned, about 2 minutes. Add shrimps and scallops and sauté until just cooked, about 3 minutes. Stir in lobster claws and return to serving temperature. Add herbs, lemon juice and season with salt and pepper.

CORN AND LOBSTER CHOWDER

DEVLIN'S COUNTRY BISTRO, MT. PLEASANT, ONTARIO

This unique version from Sous-Chef John Crowley of Devlin's Country Bistro incorporates corn, jalapeño chili and cayenne pepper to make a soup with a "bite".

2 quarts	water	2 L
1 tsp	salt	5 mL
1-2 tsp	seafood base	5-10 mL
3	ears corn, shucked	3
1½ lb	live lobster	750 g
2 tbsp	butter	30 mL
1	stalk celery, chopped	1
1 cup	diced onion	250 mL
2-3 tsp	minced jalapeño pepper	10-15 mL
2	cloves garlic, minced	2
2½ tbsp	all-purpose flour	35 mL
1½ cups	diced potato	375 mL
1 cup	heavy cream (35% M.F.)	250 mL
3-4 tsp	lemon juice	15-20 mL
pinch	cayenne pepper	
salt and pepper to taste		

In a large saucepan, bring water, salt and seafood base to boil. Add corn and lobster; cover, return to a boil and cook 15 minutes. Remove lobster and corn; quickly cool under cold running water. Remove lobster meat from shells and dice. Cut corn from cobs; reserve meat and corn.

Place lobster shells, corn cobs and juices in cooking liquid. Simmer uncovered for 30 minutes or until liquid is reduced to 1 quart (1 L). Strain stock through a fine mesh sieve lined with cheesecloth; reserve stock and discard shells and cobs.

Heat butter in a saucepan over medium heat; sauté onion, celery, jalapeño and garlic until soft, about 7 minutes. Sprinkle flour over vegetables and stir constantly; cook 1 minute. Whisk stock and cream into vegetable mixture; add potato, cover and simmer about 15 minutes or until potato is cooked. Add corn, lobster meat and lemon juice. Adjust seasoning with cayenne, salt and pepper.

Ladle in warmed soup bowls and garnish with touch of cayenne.

Serves 4 to 6

NEW ENGLAND STYLE CLAM CHOWDER

MICHAEL'S OFF BRADLEY, LONDON, ONTARIO

At Michael's Off Bradley, Executive Chef Patrick Barten adds pure maple syrup to his clam chowder, giving it a slightly sweet flavour. He chooses long, white-fleshed potato varieties, such as Shepody or Russet Burbank, for their high starch content.

3	slices bacon,	3
	(cooked crisp and crumbled)	
2 tbsp	butter	30 mL
1 cup	diced Spanish onion	250 mL
2 stalks	celery, finely diced	2
⅔ cup	finely diced carrot	150 mL
1½ cups	diced potato	375 mL
4 cups	fish stock	1 L
1/2 cup	heavy cream (35% M.F.)	125 mL
2 lbs	fresh clams, cooked & shelled	1 kg
	OR 10 oz (284 g) can whole clams	
⅛ tsp	vanilla	0.7 mL
1 tbsp	pure maple syrup	15 mL
4 tbsp	softened butter	60 mL
6 tbsp	all-purpose flour	90 mL
salt and pepper to taste		

Cook bacon until crisp; drain, crumble and set aside. In a large saucepan, melt butter over medium heat. Sauté onion, celery, carrot and potato until vegetables are transparent, about 10 minutes. Stir in crumbled bacon.

In a separate saucepan, bring the fish stock, heavy cream and clam liquid to a simmer. Stir in vanilla and maple syrup and add to vegetable mixture. Return to a simmer and cook, covered, about 10 minutes.

In a small bowl, knead softened butter and flour together and form into small balls. Stir into soup, one at a time, and continue to simmer until vegetables are cooked and soup reaches desired thickness. Stir in clams; return to serving temperature and adjust seasoning with salt and pepper.

Serves 6.

CHANTERELLE AND SCALLOP CHOWDER

KINGFISHER RESORT & SPA, ROYSTON, BC

The chefs at Kingfisher Resort and Spa highlight Pacific Northwest cuisine in their Vancouver Island restaurant overlooking Georgia Strait. This special chowder features local Qualicum Beach swimming scallops and wild Denman Island chanterelle mushrooms.

12 oz	chanterelle mushrooms	375 g
1 tbsp	olive oil	15 mL
2 tsp	minced lemon grass, (white part only)	10 mL
⅔ cup	diced sweet onion	150 mL
1 tsp	minced garlic	5 mL
½ tsp	sambal oelek* (or to taste)	2 mL
1 tsp	minced ginger root	5 mL
1	medium carrot, diced	1
1	stalk celery, diced	1
1	leek, chopped (white part only)	1
½ cup	diced celeriac	125 mL
⅓ cup	diced red pepper	75 mL
2 ½ lb	swimming scallops, in shells, cleaned OR ¾ lb (375 g) deep-sea scallops, in bite-size pieces if large	1250 g
1 tbsp	brandy	15 mL
½ cup	white wine	125 mL
1 tbsp	cornstarch	15 mL
4 cups	fish stock	1 L
1 large	Yukon Gold potato, (peeled cut in small-dice)	1
½ tsp	fish sauce**	2 mL
1 ½ tsp	ground cumin	7 mL
1 tbsp	chopped parsley	15 mL
2 tsp	chopped cilantro	10 mL
½ cup	heavy cream (35% M.F.)	125 mL

salt and pepper to taste

Clean mushrooms; split and cut in bite-sized pieces; reserve. Heat oil in a large saucepan over medium heat. Sauté lemon grass, onion, garlic, sambal oelek and ginger root for 2 minutes, stirring constantly. Add carrot, celery, leek, celeriac and red pepper; reduce heat to low, cover and cook for 5 minutes. Raise heat to medium-high; add swimming scallops and flambé with brandy. When flames cease, deglaze with wine; cover and steam scallops until shells open, about 8 minutes.

Remove scallops from saucepan and cool. When cool enough to handle, remove scallop meat from shells and reserve.

Dilute cornstarch in one cup of the fish stock and reserve. Return the saucepan with vegetables to heat; add remaining fish stock, potatoes, fish sauce and cumin. Bring to a simmer; cover and cook until potatoes are tender. Stir in cornstarch mixture and simmer 2 minutes, stirring constantly. Add reserved scallop meat, parsley and cilantro. Add cream and adjust seasoning with salt and pepper.

Serves 4 to 6

* Sambal oelek, an Indonesian condiment made with chilies, brown sugar and salt, can be found in the international food section of most supermarkets.

** Fish sauce can be found in the international food section of most supermarkets.

CURRIED MUSSEL SOUP WITH TOMATO CONCASSE

THE OBAN INN, NIAGARA-ON-THE-LAKE, ONTARIO

Chef de Cuisine Bruce Worden tells us that, "Green curry paste, especially brands available in supermarkets, goes a long way in the heat department." He advises using a small amount, increasing only if you desire a "hotter" soup.

At the Oban Inn, this chowder is served with warm, homemade herb bread.

2 lb	fresh mussels	1 kg
1 cup	dry white wine	250 mL
2 tsp	olive oil	10 mL
1	medium onion, diced	1
2	stalks celery, diced	2
1	leek, white part only, sliced	1
3	cloves garlic, minced	3
1	stalk lemon grass	1
1-2 tsp	green curry paste, to taste	5-10 mL
1 lb	Yukon gold potatoes, peeled and diced in large pieces	500 g
4 cups	fish stock	1 L
⅓ cup	heavy cream (35% M.F.)	75 mL
2-3 tbsp	lemon juice	30-45 mL
	salt and pepper to taste	
	Tomato Concasse (recipe follows)	

Scrub and debeard mussels, discarding ones that do not close when lightly tapped or have broken shells. Heat wine in a large saucepan over medium-high heat; add mussels. Bring to steaming point. Cover and cook until mussels fully open, about 6 to 7 minutes. Drain through a fine mesh strainer, reserving cooking liquid. Discard any mussels that do not open. Remove meat from shells and reserve.

Heat olive oil in the large saucepan over medium-low heat. Add onion, celery, leek and garlic. Cook covered, until onion is softened but not coloured, about 12 minutes. Stir occasionally.

Peel outer layer from lemon grass and trim ends; smash stalk with back of a knife blade to release flavour. Add lemon grass and curry paste to onion mixture; stir and cook an additional 2 minutes.

Add potato, stirring until warmed; add stock and reserved mussel liquid. Cover and simmer until potatoes are tender, about 20 minutes.

In a blender, puree soup in batches until smooth and creamy. Return to saucepan, add cream and reserved mussel meat; bring to serving temperature. Adjust seasoning with lemon juice, salt and pepper.

To serve, ladle chowder in warmed bowls and garnish with a large spoonful of Tomato Concasse in centre of soup.

Serves 6

TOMATO CONCASSE

½ lb	Yukon gold potatoes, (peeled and diced)	250 g
2	Roma tomatoes, diced	2
2 tbsp	chopped cilantro	30 mL
salt and pepper to taste		

In a saucepan, combine diced potatoes with enough cold water to cover and bring to a boil. Reduce to simmer and cook until potatoes are tender. Drain and let potatoes "air dry" to room temperature.

In a bowl, combine potato, tomato and cilantro and stir to blend. Adjust seasoning with salt and pepper and reserve for garnish.

Courgette, Brie and Chive Bisque

Bisques

This section contains a delicious selection of bisques created with a wide variety of ingredients. The most notable characteristic of these soups is that their subtle flavour is never overpowering, making them an ideal first course.

You won't be able to refuse a second serving of rich Chestnut Bisque from Vineland Estates Winery Restaurant in Ontario or Chef Marcel Kauer's Caramelized Onion and Apple Bisque from Hastings House in British Columbia.

COURGETTE, BRIE AND CHIVE BISQUE

GLENERIN INN, MISSISSAUGA, ONTARIO

Choose small courgettes or zucchini when making this bisque. The addition of Brie thickens the soup and allows the gentle flavours of the lemon and vegetables to emerge. Chef Stephen Vaughan serves his soup in warm bowls with crusty bread and a garnish of crème fraîche.

2 tbsp	butter	30 mL
1½ lb	small courgette (zucchini), sliced	750 g
¼ lb	white onion, diced	125 g
1	leek, white part only,	1
	cleaned and sliced	1
1	stalk celery, sliced	1
1	small potato, peeled and chopped	1
1	large garlic clove, crushed	1
6 cups	chicken stock	1.5 L
4 oz	Danish Brie cheese,	125 g
	(chopped with skin on)	
½	lemon, zest and juice	½
pinch	ground nutmeg	
pinch	cayenne pepper	
⅓ cup	chives, chopped	75 mL
salt and pepper to taste		
crème fraîche as garnish		

Heat butter in a heavy bottomed saucepan. Add courgette, onion, leek and celery. Sauté, stirring often, until softened, about 4 to 5 minutes. Add potato, garlic and chicken stock; cover and simmer about 15 to 20 minutes. Add Brie and whisk until melted.

In a blender, puree soup in batches until smooth. If necessary, strain through a sieve. Return soup to heat; add lemon juice and zest, nutmeg, cayenne pepper and chives. Adjust seasoning with salt and pepper. Serve with a dollop of crème fraîche.

Serves 6

CARAMELIZED ONION & APPLE BISQUE

HASTINGS HOUSE, SALT SPRING ISLAND, BC

Lovers of traditional French onion soups will adore this creamy variation. Imagine caramelized onions and sweet apples seasoned with a hint of rosemary, and then pureed into a smooth bisque. It is heavenly.

For a more pungent apple flavour, Executive Chef Marcel Kauer suggests that you replace up to 1 cup of the stock with apple juice or apple cider.

4 tbsp	butter	60 mL
2	large onions, thinly sliced	2
1	clove garlic, minced	1
1	bay leaf	1
3	medium summer apples, cored, peeled and chopped (Gravenstein, Gala, McIntosh, Granny Smith etc.)	3
1 sprig	rosemary (½ tsp/2 mL dried)	1
6 cups	vegetable or chicken stock	1.5 L
2 tbsp	all-purpose flour dissolved in 4 tbsp/60 mL cold water	30 mL
salt and pepper to taste		
½ cup	heavy cream (35% M.F.)	125 mL

Melt butter in a heavy saucepan over low heat. Sauté onions until translucent, about 10 minutes. Increase heat to medium-high; stir and cook until onions are evenly browned. Be careful not to burn.

Add garlic, rosemary, bay leaf, apples and stock and bring to a boil. Reduce heat, cover, and simmer 30 to 40 minutes.

In a blender, puree soup in batches until smooth and creamy. Return soup to saucepan and gently reheat. If soup needs to be thickened, whisk in enough flour mixture to reach desired consistency and simmer for 4 minutes. Adjust seasoning with salt and pepper.

Serves 6

SMOKED HADDOCK BISQUE WITH PEAR AND SEARED SCALLOPS

RESTAURANT LES FOUGÈRES, CHELSEA, QUÉBEC

Chefs Jennifer and Charles Part combine the flavours of smoked haddock with fresh pears and curry in this magnificent bisque. They garnish their creation with seared sea scallops, orange segments, coriander sprigs and orange zest.

8 oz	smoked haddock fillet	250 g
1	small onion, chopped	1
1	small poached pear, chopped*	1
2 tbsp	butter, divided	30 mL
2 tsp	curry powder	10 mL
1	large potato, peeled and coarsely chopped	1
3 cups	chicken stock	750 mL
1 cup	pear juice or nectar	250 mL
2 tbsp	heavy cream (35% M.F.)	30 mL
2 tsp	frozen orange juice concentrate	10 mL
salt and pepper to taste		
12	small sea scallops, rinsed and patted dry	12
4	orange segments, peeled and pith removed	4
fresh coriander sprigs		
1 tsp	orange zest	5 mL

Refresh smoked haddock with several changes of cold water. Carefully remove bones and any attached skin. Break into bite-sized pieces.

Sauté onion and pear in 1 tbsp (15 mL) butter until onion is translucent. Add haddock, curry powder, potato, stock and pear juice. Simmer until potato is soft, about 15 to 20 minutes.

In a blender, puree mixture until smooth and creamy. Return soup to a clean pot. Stir in cream and orange juice concentrate. Reheat gently; be careful not to boil. Adjust seasoning with salt and pepper. Keep warm.

Melt 1 tbsp (15 mL) butter in a skillet over high heat. Sear scallops on one side only, until caramelized.

Divide soup among four bowls and garnish with 3 scallops, caramelized side up, an orange segment, coriander sprig and a sprinkle of orange zest.

Serves 4

* To poach pear: Bring ¾ cup (175 mL) water and ¼ cup (50 mL) sugar to a boil. Add 2 to 3 slices lemon and 1 coin-sized piece of peeled fresh ginger. Add peeled and cored pear quarters and simmer until tender.

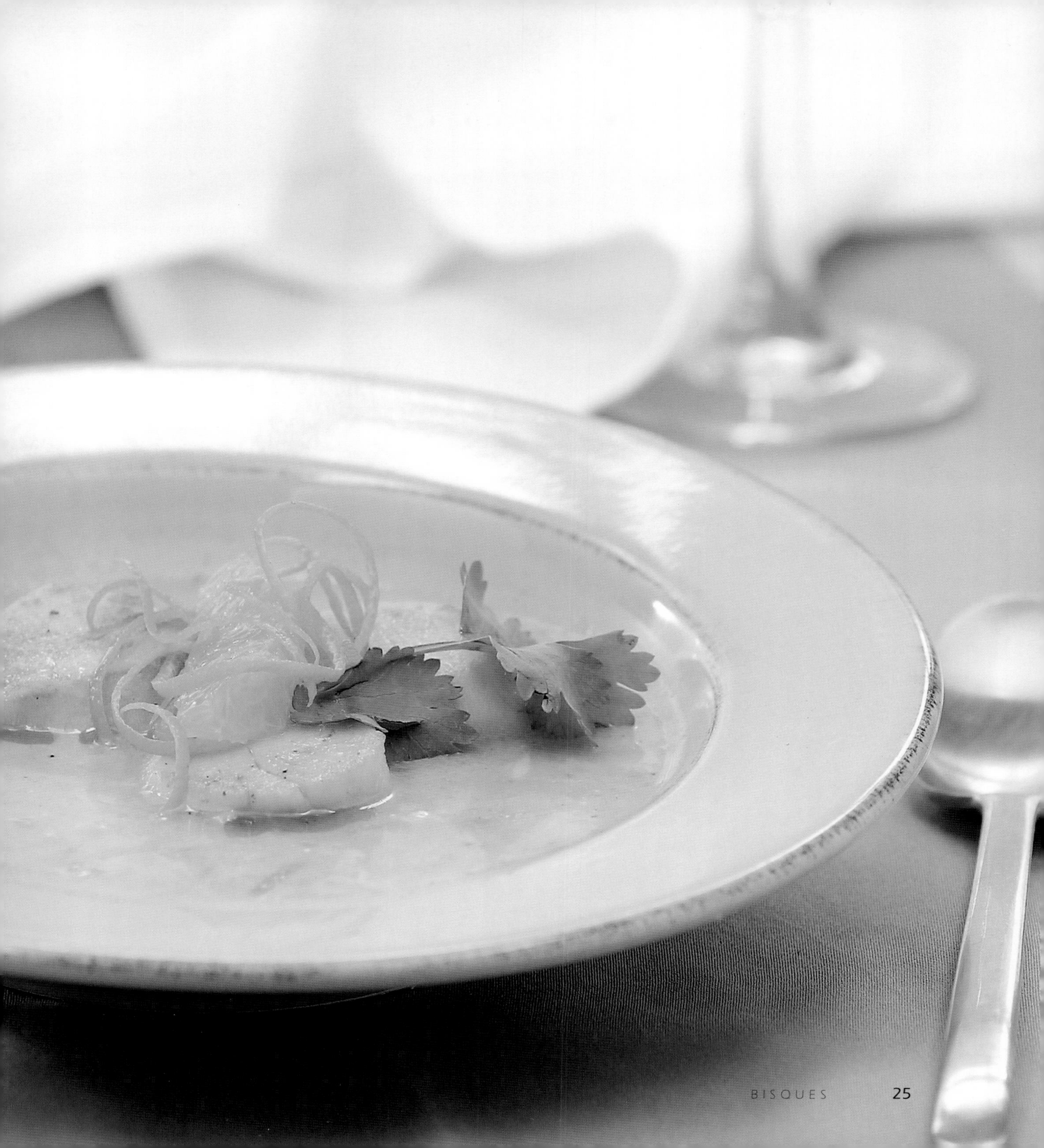

LOBSTER BISQUE CAPPUCCINO

DIVA AT THE MET, VANCOUVER, BC

Executive Chef Scott Baechler serves his lobster bisque in demitasse or cappuccino cups topped with foamed milk and a dusting of Chinese five-spice powder. How elegant!

2 lb	cooked, lobster bodies and claw shells	1 kg
3 tbsp	butter	45 mL
1½ cups	chopped onion	375 mL
⅓ cup	brandy	75 mL
⅔ cup	white wine	150 mL
⅓ cup	tomato paste	75 mL
2 tbsp	all-purpose flour	30 mL
3 cups	heavy cream (35% M.F.)	750 mL
3 cups	fish stock	750 mL
salt and white pepper to taste		
1 cup	foamed milk	250 mL
Chinese five-spice powder		

Remove the lobsters' sand sacs (the organ located behind the eyes); break up lobster bodies and claws into medium-sized pieces.

Heat butter in a large saucepan over medium-low heat. Add lobster shells and onion; sauté, stirring frequently, until onion is very soft, about 12 minutes.

Increase heat to medium and deglaze pan with brandy; ignite the pan's contents. When flames die, add white wine and stir well. Add tomato paste and cook, stirring frequently, about 4 minutes. Sprinkle flour over mixture; whisk to combine and cook, stirring constantly, about 2 minutes.

Add cream and fish stock. Bring to a simmer, cover and cook 30 minutes, stirring occasionally. Strain through a fine mesh strainer. Return bisque to saucepan; adjust seasoning with salt and pepper and keep warm.

Foam milk with a cappuccino frother (optional). Ladle bisque into cappuccino cups and crown with a dollop of foamed milk. Finish each serving with a fine dusting of Chinese five-spice powder. Serve immediately.

Serves 6

CHESTNUT BISQUE

VINELAND ESTATES WINERY RESTAURANT,
VINELAND, ONTARIO

Executive Chef Mark Picone cautions that many Canadian chestnuts are not suitable for human consumption, however, in the Niagara Peninsula, edible chestnuts can be purchased from some local growers. Imported chestnuts are readily available in most grocery stores from late fall until Christmas.

1 tbsp	olive oil	15 mL
1	large onion, diced	1
2	medium carrots, diced	2
1 lb	celeriac (celery root), diced	500 g
8 cups	chicken stock	2 L
1	large bay leaf	1
1 lb	chestnuts, roasted and peeled*	500 g
1 cup	heavy cream (35% M.F.)	250 mL
salt and pepper to taste		
4 oz	foie gras, cut in small cubes (optional)	120 g
honey for garnish (preferably organic)		

Heat olive oil in large saucepan over medium heat. Sauté onion, carrots and celeriac until vegetables are slightly softened, about 10 minutes. Stir frequently; do not allow vegetables to brown. Add chicken stock, bay leaf and chestnuts; simmer until vegetables and chestnuts are soft, about 30 to 40 minutes.

In a blender, puree soup in batches until smooth and creamy. If needed, strain through a fine mesh sieve. Return soup to saucepan and adjust seasoning with salt and pepper. Reheat gently and just before serving, add cream and foie gras (optional). The bisque should have a pea soup consistency.

Ladle into cream soup bowls and drizzle a small amount of honey over top.

Serves 6 to 8

* To roast chestnuts: Score chestnuts with an "X." Be sure to cut through the tough shell. Place nuts on a baking sheet and roast in a preheated 350°F (180°C) oven for 25 minutes. The "X" will slightly peel back. Remove from oven and as soon as they are cool enough to handle, peel the shells. Chop chestnuts and reserve.

ALMOND BISQUE

KELTIC LODGE, INGONISH BEACH, NS

The subtle flavour of this creamy white bisque makes a pleasant prelude to a dinner entrée.

½ cup	whole blanched almonds	125 mL
6 cups	chicken stock	1.5 L
¼ cup	long-grain rice	50 mL
1	medium leek, white part only, chopped	1
¼ cup	heavy cream (35% M.F.)	50 mL
3	egg yolks	3
salt and white pepper to taste		
1-2 tbsp	Amaretto liqueur	15-30 mL
⅓ cup	sliced almonds, toasted*	75 mL

Bring whole almonds, stock, rice and chopped leek to a boil in a heavy-bottomed saucepan. Reduce heat, cover and simmer until almonds are tender, about 45 to 55 minutes.

In a blender, puree soup in batches until smooth and creamy.

In a small bowl, whisk together cream and egg yolks. Return bisque to saucepan and bring to a near boil. Add cream and egg yolk mixture, stirring constantly. Cook for 1 minute, be careful not to boil.

Season to taste with salt, white pepper and Amaretto. Return to blender and puree to a smooth, creamy texture.

Serve in cream soup bowls. Garnish with toasted almonds.

Serves 6

* To toast almonds, preheat oven to 350°F (180°C). Spread almond slices on a baking sheet and bake, watching closely, until golden brown, about 4 to 5 minutes.

Chilled Sweet Pea, Mint and Yogurt Soup

Chilled Soups

Whether you decide to dine on the patio or take a chilled soup on an elegant picnic, these recipes are ideally suited to al fresco dining. Here, we offer traditional soups such as Summer Gazpacho with Roasted Corn and Crab Salsa, from Chef Chris Helmer of the Teahouse Restaurant and Chilled Vichyssoise with Smoked Salmon and Dill from Chef Eric Madden at Beild House Country.

Be sure to sample Chef Drew Rudderham's Sweet Pea, Mint and Yogurt Soup which combines the best of summer's bounty or Chilled Raspberry Soup from Chef Rory Golden at Deerhurst Resort in Ontario. Prepare these refreshing soups early in the day so that the flavours fuse before serving.

CHILLED SWEET PEA, MINT AND YOGURT SOUP

ACTON'S GRILL AND CAFÉ, WOLFVILLE, NS

Fresh green peas and mint flavour this delightful soup – a perfect pick for a summer's day. Owner and Chef Drew Rudderham suggests preparing this soup one day in advance to allow the flavours to blend.

2 cups	sweet onions, chopped	500 mL
1 cup	fresh mint leaves, chopped	250 mL
2 tbsp	vegetable oil	30 mL
2 cups	fresh or frozen green peas	500 mL
4 cups	chicken stock	1 L
2 cups	plain yogurt	500 mL
6 drops	Tabasco sauce	6

Sauté onions and mint in oil over medium heat until onions are caramelized, about 12 minutes. Stir in peas and chicken stock. Bring to a boil; reduce heat and simmer 10 minutes or until peas are tender. Cool slightly and puree in a blender.

Once soup is at room temperature, stir in yogurt and Tabasco sauce. Cover and refrigerate at least 8 hours.

Serves 4 to 6

CHILLED BLUEBERRY SOUP

THE BLOMIDON INN, WOLFVILLE, NS

Blueberries have been designated the official berry of Nova Scotia. The chefs at the Blomidon Inn have chosen this versatile fruit as the main ingredient in this delightful chilled soup.

2 cups	blueberries	500 mL
¾ cup	sour cream or plain yogurt	175 mL
¾ cup	champagne	175 mL
1 cup	blend (12% M.F.)	250 mL
1½ tsp	cassis liqueur	7 mL
½ tsp	lemon juice	2 mL

whipped cream (35% M.F.) as garnish
fresh mint leaves as garnish

Combine blueberries, sour cream, champagne, blend, cassis and lemon juice in a food processor or blender; puree until smooth.

Serve in chilled bowls with a dollop of whipped cream and fresh mint leaves.

Serves 4

SUMMER RASPBERRY SOUP

DEERHURST RESORT, HUNTSVILLE, ONTARIO

This rich, lush fruity soup will delight your senses. At Deerhurst Resort, Executive Chef Rory Golden serves his refreshing soup in ice bowls. Chef Golden says, "It is imperative to have all ingredients chilled before preparation."

1 qt	fresh or frozen raspberries (reserve a few for garnish)	1 L
1 cup	apple juice	250 mL
¾ cup	milk (2% to 3.5% M.F.)	175 mL
¼ tsp	cinnamon	1 mL
1	McIntosh apple, peeled, cored & cut into ¼-inch (0.5 cm) pieces	1
¾ cup	raspberry yogurt	175 mL
2 tbsp	pure maple syrup	30 mL
1 cup	sparkling water	250 mL
4	mint sprigs for garnish	4

In a chilled stainless steel bowl, crush raspberries. Add apple juice, milk and cinnamon and whisk to combine. Chill 15 minutes.

Pour soup through a sieve to remove seeds. Add apple, yogurt and maple syrup to soup; adjust flavour with additional maple syrup and cinnamon if necessary.

Ladle soup into 4 cold bowls adding ¼ cup (50 mL) sparkling water to each bowl before serving (this may be done at the dinner table). Garnish with fresh raspberries and mint sprigs.

Serves 4

CHILLED BING CHERRY SOUP

EDGEWATER MANOR RESTAURANT, STONEY
CREEK, ONTARIO

Edgewater Manor Restaurant is fortunate to be
located in one of the prime fruit-farming regions
of Canada. Chef Terry Terpoy loves to incorporate
the "best produce of the season" in his recipes.
You will love the wonderful flavour and beautiful
presentation of this soup.

Choose plump and juicy, dark red to black
sweet cherries.

1½ lb	pitted cherries	750 g
2 cups	apple juice	500 mL
1½ tbsp	fresh lemon juice	20 mL
½ cup	honey	125 mL
2	cloves	2
1	medium cinnamon stick	1
½ cup	white wine	125 mL

plain yogurt
slivered almonds, toasted* (see page 29)

Combine cherries, apple juice, lemon juice,
honey, cloves and cinnamon stick in a large
saucepan. Bring to a boil; reduce heat and
simmer for 20 to 30 minutes until cherries are
tender. Discard cloves and cinnamon stick.

In a blender, puree soup in batches until smooth.
If necessary, strain the puree through a fine sieve
to remove pulp.

Stir wine into soup and ladle into chilled bowls.
Garnish bowls with a dollop of yogurt and a
sprinkling of toasted almonds.

Serves 6

CHILLED SENEGALESE PEANUT SOUP

THE WINDSOR HOUSE OF ST. ANDREWS,
ST. ANDREWS-BY-THE-SEA, NB

Blessed is the chef with a pot of fresh herbs on his doorstep! At the Windsor House of St. Andrews, Chef Peter Woodworth garnishes this spicy soup with a sprinkling of freshly picked cilantro.

2 tbsp	*peanut or olive oil*	*30 mL*
1	*medium Spanish onion, chopped*	*1*
2	*cloves garlic, minced*	*2*
¾ tsp	*cayenne pepper*	*3 mL*
1½-2 tsp	*curry powder, or to taste*	*7-10 mL*
3 cups	*chicken stock*	*750 mL*
¾ cup	*peanuts (or ½ cup/125 mL of smooth peanut butter)*	*175 mL*
6	*tomatoes, seeded and coarsely chopped (or 3½ cups/875mL drained and seeded canned tomatoes, chopped)*	*6*

salt and freshly ground pepper to taste
fresh cilantro, chopped

Heat oil in a large heavy-bottomed pot over medium-low heat. Add onion, garlic and cayenne pepper; sauté for 10 minutes, stirring frequently. Stir in curry powder and add chicken stock, peanuts or peanut butter and chopped tomatoes.

Simmer soup in a covered saucepan for 20 minutes or until vegetables are soft.

In a blender, puree soup until smooth and then strain through a medium mesh strainer, pushing on vegetables with a ladle.

Let soup chill several hours before serving. Adjust seasoning with salt and freshly ground pepper and garnish with a sprinkling of freshly chopped cilantro.

Serves 6

CHILLED VICHYSSOISE WITH SMOKED SALMON AND DILL

BEILD HOUSE COUNTRY INN, COLLINGWOOD, ONTARIO

This elegant soup calls for thinly sliced smoked salmon prepared by the "cold smoked" process. At Beild House, Chef Eric Madden suggests preparing the soup one day in advance to allow the flavours to blend. He serves this soup accompanied by a glass of Riesling wine.

1 tbsp	butter	15 mL
1	large carrot, peeled and diced	1
1	stalk celery, diced	1
1	clove garlic, minced	1
1	small onion, diced	1
1	large potato, peeled and diced	1
3 cups	chicken or vegetable stock	750 mL
1 cup	whole milk unflavoured yogurt	250 mL
4 oz	cold-smoked salmon, thinly sliced	125 g
¼ cup	chopped fresh dill	50 mL

Heat butter in a saucepan over medium-low heat. Add carrots, celery, garlic and onion; cover and cook until soft, about 10 minutes. Stir in potato and stock; continue to cook until potatoes are soft.

Cool slightly and puree until smooth in a blender. Stir in yogurt and dill; cover and refrigerate 8 hours.

Ladle into chilled bowls and float thin slices of salmon on top. Garnish with a sprig of fresh dill.

Serves 4

ICED MELON SOUP

L'EUROPE INN & RESTAURANT,
ST. ANDREWS-BY-THE-SEA, NB

Chef Markus Ritter suggests that you purchase
firm melons and then allow them to ripen and
sweeten at room temperature for a few days.

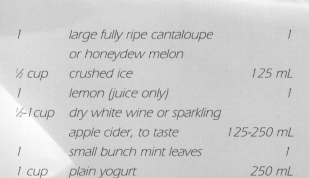

1	large fully ripe cantaloupe or honeydew melon	1
½ cup	crushed ice	125 mL
1	lemon (juice only)	1
½-1 cup	dry white wine or sparkling apple cider, to taste	125-250 mL
1	small bunch mint leaves	1
1 cup	plain yogurt	250 mL

Peel melon; cut in half and remove seeds. Dice
melon and puree with crushed ice in a food
processor or blender. Transfer to a large bowl, stir
in lemon juice and wine or cider.

Using a sharp knife, slice 6 to 8 mint leaves into
slivers and stir into soup. Refrigerate until very
cold.

Ladle soup into chilled bowls; add 2 tablespoons
(30 mL) of yogurt to each serving and swirl.
Garnish with fresh mint leaves.

Serves 6

SUMMER GAZPACHO WITH ROASTED CORN & CRAB SALSA

THE TEAHOUSE RESTAURANT, KELOWNA, BC

The addition of hot, smoky chipotle peppers and fresh lime juice gives this summertime soup a "cool-with-a-bite" taste. It is essential to use fresh vine-ripened tomatoes for optimum flavour and consistency.

2	red peppers	2
6	large, vine-ripened tomatoes	6
3	medium cucumbers, peeled and seeded	3
1	red onion, peeled and quartered	1
3	cloves garlic, minced	3
¼ cup	fresh parsley	50 mL
¼ cup	fresh cilantro	50 mL
1-2	chipotle peppers (canned in adobo sauce, or dried)	1-2
2	limes, zest and juice	2
¼ cup	extra virgin olive oil	50 mL

salt and pepper to taste
Roasted Corn and Crab Salsa (recipe follows)

On a baking sheet, roast whole red peppers in a preheated 400°F oven for 20 to 25 minutes; turning 2 to 3 times until skin is charred. Remove from oven and place peppers in a sealed plastic or paper bag until cool. When cool enough to handle, slide charred skin from peppers; core and remove seeds and membrane.

In a pot of boiling water, blanch tomatoes for 30 seconds; remove and plunge in ice water to shock. Remove skins and seeds from tomatoes.

Combine all ingredients, except salt, pepper and salsa, in a food processor and blend until almost smooth. Pour into a large bowl; adjust seasoning with salt and pepper. If necessary, adjust consistency with cold water or tomato juice. Refrigerate for several hours to blend flavours.

Ladle in soup bowls and top with Roasted Corn and Crab Salsa.

Serves 6

ROASTED CORN AND CRAB SALSA

This salsa is also a delicious accompaniment to grilled seafood.

2	ears of corn, shucked	2
1-2 tsp	vegetable oil	5-10 mL
1	red pepper, cut into small pieces	1
¼ cup	chopped green onion	50 mL
¼ cup	chopped cilantro	50 mL
1-2 tbsp	extra virgin olive oil	15-30 mL
2-3 tbsp	rice vinegar	30-45 mL
½ cup	crab meat, fresh or canned	125 mL

salt and pepper to taste

Brush corn with oil; grill or roast in preheated 400ºF oven until cooked and golden brown. Cool corn and remove the kernels.

In a bowl, combine corn, red pepper, green onion, cilantro, olive oil, rice vinegar and crab meat. Adjust seasoning with salt and pepper. Refrigerate for at least 30 minutes to blend flavours.

Makes 3 cups (750 mL) salsa

Carrot, Orange and Ginger Soup

Creamed Soups

In this section you will find some of the prettiest soups in our recipe collection. Vibrant red, lush green and autumn orange allow you to freely experiment with garnishes — with a dollop of crème fraîche or perhaps an herb or spicy crouton.

These recipes take advantage of local seasonal produce, representative of each restaurant's geographic region. Chef Mary Anne Nylen from Prairie Orchard Teahouse in Manitoba celebrates spring with Cream of Asparagus Soup, made with the season's first crop of asparagus. While Café Brio's Pumpkin and Porcini Soup makes a culinary statement with colourful autumn baking pumpkins.

CARROT, ORANGE AND GINGER SOUP

BLUE GINGER LOUNGE AND GRILL, LONDON, ONTARIO

Chef William Lomas says, "This easy-to-make soup is full of interesting Asian flavours that have a perfect combination of sweet and sour. It is also light, fresh and healthy." He likes to add the orange juice at the end to keep its freshness, and often adds a shot of miso paste or sesame oil for an interesting variation.

2 tsp	olive oil	10 mL
1½ cup	diced onion	375 mL
1 cup	diced celery	250 mL
1½ cups	diced carrot	375 mL
2 tbsp	minced ginger root	30 mL
½ cup	mirin (sweet Japanese rice wine)	125 mL
5 cups	chicken or vegetable stock	1.25 L
⅔ cup	fresh orange juice	150 mL
salt and pepper to taste		
cilantro sprigs for garnish		

Heat the olive oil in a large saucepan over medium heat. Add onion, celery, carrot and ginger root; cover and cook over low heat, stirring occasionally, until onion is translucent but not browned, about 10 minutes. Add mirin and reduce by half. Add stock and simmer until vegetables are soft, about 20 minutes.

In a blender, puree soup in batches until smooth and creamy. Return to heat; add orange juice and adjust seasoning with salt and pepper.

Ladle in soup bowls and garnish with a sprig of cilantro.

Serves 6

TOMATO AND JALAPEÑO BROTH WITH ORANGE ESSENCE

THE ROUSSEAU HOUSE, ANCASTER, ONTARIO

Executive Chef Kai Bein caramelizes the onion and garlic to bring out the vegetables' natural sugars, increasing the sweetness of the soup. Look for varieties such as navel, Valencia or blood oranges because they have a sweeter, more intense flavour.

1 tbsp	olive oil	15 mL
½	large sweet onion, diced	½
2	garlic cloves, minced	2
½	small jalapeño pepper, minced	½
1	large orange, juice and zest	1
1	stalk celery, chopped	1
1 can	Italian plum tomatoes	28 oz/840 mL
4 cups	chicken stock	1 L
1 tbsp	sugar	15 mL
¾ cup	diced potato	175 mL
¼ tsp	cayenne pepper 1 mL	
¼ tsp	sweet paprika	1 mL
½ cup	heavy cream (35% M.F.)	125 mL

salt and pepper to taste

herb-flavoured croutons & snipped chives for garnish

Heat olive oil in a large saucepan over medium heat. Sauté onion and garlic until golden, stirring frequently, about 10 to 15 minutes. Add jalapeño, orange zest and celery. Reduce heat to low; cover and cook, stirring frequently until softened, about 10 minutes.

Add orange juice; raise heat to medium-high and reduce by half. Add tomatoes, stock, sugar and potatoes; bring to a simmer and cook until potatoes are cooked, about 20 minutes.

In a blender, puree soup in batches until smooth and creamy. Return soup to saucepan; add cayenne and paprika and simmer 10 minutes. Adjust seasoning with salt and pepper.

Ladle in warm soup bowls garnished with herb-flavoured croutons and snipped chives.

Serves 6

PARSLEY SOUP

LANGDON HALL, CAMBRIDGE, ONTARIO

1 tbsp	extra virgin olive oil	15 mL
⅔ cup	chopped onion	150 mL
½ cup	chopped leek, white part only	125 mL
⅔ cup	chopped fennel	150 mL
2	cloves garlic, minced	2
2	shallots, thinly sliced	2
4 cups	chicken stock	1 L
¾ cup	Yukon Gold potato, diced	175 mL
2 tsp	lemon juice	10 mL
½ cup	heavy cream (35% M.F.)	125 mL
1	large bunch parsley	1

salt to taste

Heat oil in a saucepan over medium-low heat. Add onion, leek, fennel, garlic and shallots; cover and stir frequently, until softened but not browned, about 10 minutes. Add chicken stock and potato; bring to a boil. Reduce heat, cover and simmer, about 30 minutes.

While soup is simmering, blanch parsley in boiling water for 2 minutes; drain and reserve.

In a blender, puree soup in batches until smooth and creamy. Return soup to saucepan; add cream and lemon juice and bring to serving temperature.

In a blender, puree parsley with ½ cup soup until smooth. Whisk parsley puree into soup, adjust seasoning and serve immediately.

Serves 4

CURRIED CARROT AND LEEK SOUP

THE LION INN, LUNENBURG, NS

Owner and Chef George Morin shares his quick and easy method for preparing carrot and leek soup. He uses medium curry powder and allows his soup to slowly simmer to perfection.

2	medium leeks, white and pale green parts only, chopped	2
1 lb	carrots, peeled and diced	500 g
½ tsp	medium curry powder	2 mL
5 cups	chicken stock	1.25 L

salt and pepper to taste
croutons as garnish

Trim and carefully wash ends and tops of leeks. In a saucepan, combine leeks, carrots, curry powder and stock and bring to a boil. Reduce heat; cover and simmer until vegetables are soft, about 25 minutes.

In a blender, puree soup in batches until smooth and creamy. Return to saucepan, adjust seasoning with salt and pepper; return to serving temperature.

Ladle in soup bowls and garnish with croutons.

Serves 4 to 6

CREAM OF BROCCOLI & CELERY SOUP

SANDWICH PATCH CAFÉ,
NORTH BATTLEFORD, SASKATCHEWAN

This soup is a perfect first course for entertaining. Creamy and rich, yet delicate in flavour, it complements and never overpowers the entrée course.

1	large bunch broccoli, florets and tender stalk, roughly chopped	1
2 cups	diced celery	500 mL
1 cup	diced onion	250 mL
4 cups	chicken stock	1 L
1 cup	heavy cream (35% M.F.)	250 mL
1 tbsp	chopped tarragon (1 tsp/5 mL dried)	15 mL
salt and white pepper to taste		
6 oz	cream cheese, cubed	180 g

In a large saucepan, combine broccoli, celery, onion and stock. Bring to a boil; reduce heat to medium, cover and simmer until vegetables are soft, about 15 minutes.

In a blender, puree soup in batches. If needed, strain through a fine mesh sieve to remove any small pieces of celery.

Return soup to saucepan over medium-low heat; add cream and tarragon. Adjust seasoning with salt and pepper. Add cream cheese and stir constantly until cheese is melted and soup is creamy.

Ladle soup into warmed bowls and garnish with freshly chopped tarragon.

Serves 6

CELERIAC & GINGER SOUP WITH PROSCIUTTO & FRESH PARMESAN

BEILD HOUSE COUNTRY INN,
COLLINGWOOD, ONTARIO

This pureed vegetable soup achieves elegant status with the addition of very thin slices of Italian prosciutto ham and freshly grated Parmesan cheese. Executive Chef Eric Madden finishes his presentation with a twist from his pepper mill, which "completes the fragrance from the bowl."

4 tbsp	unsalted butter	60 mL
1 lb	celeriac (celery root), peeled and chopped	500 g
1	onion, chopped	1
1-inch	piece fresh ginger root, peeled and sliced	2.5 cm
1	garlic clove, minced	1
6 cups	chicken stock	1.5 L
2	medium potatoes, peeled and cubed	2

salt and pepper to taste
heavy cream (35% M.F.), as needed to thin soup

4 oz	prosciutto ham, thinly sliced	125 g

fresh Parmesan cheese for grating
ground pepper

Melt butter in a large saucepan over low heat. Add celeriac, onion, ginger root and garlic; cook on low heat with lid on, for about 15 minutes, or until soft. Add chicken stock and potatoes. Bring to a boil; reduce heat to simmer and cook until potatoes are soft, about 20 minutes.

In a blender, puree soup in batches until smooth and creamy. Return soup to saucepan; adjust seasoning with salt and pepper and thin consistency with heavy cream, if necessary.

Ladle soup in warmed bowls and garnish with prosciutto on top. Grate Parmesan cheese on the prosciutto and top with freshly ground pepper.

Serves 6

CREAM OF ASPARAGUS SOUP

PRAIRIE ORCHARD TEA HOUSE,
NEEPAWA, MANITOBA

At the Prairie Orchard Tea House, all produce is organically grown as Chef Mary Anne Nylen believes this provides the best nutritional value and flavour. She suggests serving this soup with warm cheddar scones.

3 tbsp	butter	45 mL
2	cloves garlic, crushed	2
4 tbsp	all-purpose flour	60 mL
6 cups	chicken stock,	1.5 L
1 lb	asparagus, trimmed and cut in 1-inch (2.5 cm) pieces	500g
1 cup	sour cream	250 mL
2 tbsp	cornstarch	30 mL
3 tbsp	fresh dill weed, (2-3 tsp/10-15 mL dried)	45 mL

salt and pepper to taste

Melt butter in a large saucepan over medium-low heat. Add garlic and sauté; be careful not to brown. Add flour and whisk into garlic mixture. Whisk in 1 cup (250 mL) of chicken stock to form a smooth paste.

Gradually add remaining stock, one cup at a time; bring to a boil after each addition. Stir in asparagus, return to a simmer and cook until asparagus is tender but still crisp, about 4 minutes.

In a separate bowl, combine sour cream and cornstarch. Stir in a small amount of hot mixture, then add to soup and cook 3 minutes; stir constantly until soup is thickened. Add dill and adjust seasoning with salt and pepper.

Serves 6

ROASTED RED PEPPER, SWEET POTATO AND MELON SOUP

THE DUNDEE ARMS, CHARLOTTETOWN, PEI

Roasting red peppers brings out an intense flavour quite different from the raw vegetable. In this delightful soup, Chef Patrick Young combines roasted vegetables with sweet honeydew melon. He advises that a little cream may be added if a richer soup is desired.

2	red peppers	2
½	large Spanish onion, diced	½
1½ lb	sweet potato, peeled and diced	750 g
2 tsp	olive oil	10 mL
4 tsp	brown sugar	60 mL
¼ tsp	curry powder	1 mL
1	large clove garlic, crushed	1
½ tsp	salt	2 mL
¼ tsp	black pepper	2 mL
5 cups	chicken stock	1.25 L
¼	small honeydew melon, peeled and cubed	¼

On a baking sheet, roast whole red peppers in a preheated 400°F oven for 20 to 25 minutes; turning 2 to 3 times until skin is charred. Remove from oven and place peppers in a sealed plastic or paper bag until cool. When cool enough to handle, slide charred skin from peppers; core and remove seeds and membrane. Chop into bite-size pieces.

Combine diced onion and sweet potato and toss with olive oil. Place in a shallow baking dish and sprinkle with brown sugar, curry powder, garlic, salt and pepper. Bake in a preheated 400°F (200°C) oven until potato is tender, approximately 30 minutes.

In a large saucepan, bring chicken stock to a boil. Stir in roasted vegetables and red pepper. Reduce heat to simmer; cover and cook for 20 minutes. Remove from heat and cool.

Add melon and puree soup in a blender until smooth. Return to serving temperature and adjust seasoning.

Serves 6

PUMPKIN AND PORCINI SOUP

CAFÉ BRIO, VICTORIA, BC

You may substitute canned pumpkin for the roasted pumpkin in this recipe, but we advise taking the extra effort to prepare a fresh pumpkin. The caramelized pumpkin flavour you achieve with roasting cannot be duplicated with prepared pumpkin.

This recipe makes a substantial amount of soup. It may be halved, but we suggest making the full amount; it takes the same amount of time and leftovers can be frozen for another day.

1	medium pumpkin, (3 lb/1.5 kg)	1
1	whole garlic	1
4-5	sprigs fresh thyme (1 tsp/5 mL dried)	4-5
½ cup	butter, melted	125 mL
2 tbsp	extra virgin olive oil	30 mL
2	medium yellow onions, diced	2
½ lb	porcini mushrooms, (optional: 1 oz/30 g, dried)	250 g
2 cups	white wine	500 mL
4-5 cups	chicken or vegetable stock	1-1.25 L
1	cinnamon stick	1
pinch ground nutmeg		
salt and pepper to taste		
½ cup	heavy cream (35% M.F.)	125 mL
fresh thyme for garnish		

Cut pumpkin in wedges; peel and remove seeds and stringy pulp. Separate garlic bulb into individual cloves and peel. Toss pumpkin wedges, garlic cloves and thyme sprigs with half the melted butter. Place vegetables on a baking sheet and roast in preheated 350°F (180°C) oven; brush with remaining butter after 20 minutes. Continue baking until pumpkin is soft and begins to caramelize, an additional 15 to 20 minutes.

If using dried porcini mushrooms, re-hydrate in a bowl of lukewarm water for about 30 minutes. Drain before using.

In a large stockpot, add olive oil and onions. Sauté over medium heat until onions begin to colour, about 25 to 30 minutes. Add porcini mushrooms; reduce heat to low; cover and cook for 10 minutes. Add wine; raise heat to medium-high and reduce by half.

Add roasted pumpkin and garlic, stock, cinnamon and nutmeg. Bring to a simmer and cook until flavours have blended and all vegetables are soft. Remove cinnamon stick and puree soup in batches in a blender. Return to stockpot; add cream and gently heat; be careful not to boil. Adjust seasoning with salt and pepper.

Ladle into warmed soup bowls and garnish with a small sprig of fresh thyme.

Serves 8 to 10

ROASTED EGGPLANT SOUP WITH CORN & TOMATO SALSA GARNISH

HALLIBURTON HOUSE INN, HALIFAX, NS

Chef Scott Vail serves this "hot and spicy" creamed soup with a Southwestern-style salsa made with corn, tomatoes, fresh cilantro, lime juice and roasted jalapeño peppers. It is a great dish to serve on a chilly autumn or winter's day.

   If you feel the soup is a little too "hot" for your palate, start with 1 teaspoon of chipotle pepper, adding more if desired.

1	whole garlic, roasted, (see page 61 for recipe)	1
3 lb	eggplant	1.5 kg
¼ cup	olive oil	50 mL
2	onions, thinly sliced	2
3	shallots, thinly sliced	3
2 tsp	toasted cumin seeds,* (2 tsp/10 mL ground cumin)	10 mL
2 tsp	chopped fresh thyme (½ tsp/2 mL dried)	10 mL
2 tsp	chipotle pepper in adobo sauce	10 mL
1 cup	white wine	250 mL
5 cups	chicken stock	1.25 mL
1 cup	heavy cream (35% M.F.)	250 mL
salt and pepper to taste		
Corn & Tomato Salsa (recipe follows)		

Roast garlic according to the directions. Wash eggplant and cut in half lengthwise. Place cut side down on baking sheet and roast in preheated 350°F (180°C) oven until soft, about 20 to 25 minutes. Cool slightly and remove skin; chop pulp and reserve.

In a large saucepan, heat olive oil and sauté onions and shallots over low heat until completely soft, but not browned, about 15 minutes. Add roasted garlic, cumin, thyme and chipotle pepper to saucepan. Raise heat to medium-high; add wine and deglaze, reducing the liquid by half.

Add eggplant and chicken stock. Bring to a boil; reduce heat, cover and simmer for 20 minutes. Remove from heat; season with salt and pepper and cool for 20 minutes.

In a blender or food processor, puree soup in batches until smooth. If necessary, strain the puree through a fine sieve to ensure a smooth consistency. Return soup to a saucepan and bring back to a simmer. Whisk in cream and adjust seasoning with salt and pepper.

Serve in warmed soup bowls with a spoonful of Corn & Tomato Salsa in center.

Serves 8

Heat cumin seeds in a small skillet over medium heat. Shake skillet frequently and cook until seeds are fragrant, about 3 to 4 minutes. Cool and crush in a spice grinder or with a mortar and pestle.

CORN & TOMATO SALSA

We suggest you double or triple this recipe and use the extra as a garnish for your favorite Mexican entrée or as an accompaniment to chicken and seafood.

1 cup	fresh corn kernels	250 mL
1	jalapeño pepper, roasted	1
1 cup	tomatoes, peeled, seeded and diced	250 mL
2 tsp	chopped cilantro	10 mL
2 tsp	finely diced red onion	10 mL
2 tsp	olive oil	10 mL
1 tsp	fresh lime juice	5 mL
salt and pepper to taste		

Heat a small amount of olive oil in a skillet over medium heat. Add corn and cook; stir frequently until slightly brown and fragrant. Remove from heat and cool.

Place jalapeño pepper over an open flame or under a broiler until charred on all sides. Place pepper in a paper bag, seal and rest 10 minutes. Remove pepper from bag; peel skin, remove seeds and membrane, finely mince.

In a bowl, combine all ingredients; stir and adjust seasoning with salt and pepper. Store refrigerated, bringing to room temperature to serve.

Makes 2 cups

CREAMY SNOW PEA SOUP

RAINCITY GRILL, VANCOUVER, BC

Executive Chef Sean Cousins' Creamy Snow Pea
Soup is a culinary statement of perfect balance.
His use of delicate snow peas is complemented
by the addition of white wine, shallots and
cream, with a hint of bay.

Chef Cousins also suggests serving this soup
"chilled" during the warm weather.

1 lb	snow peas (optional: ½ lb/250 g	500 g
	frozen petits pois)	
3 tbsp	butter	45 mL
5	shallots, finely sliced	5
3	cloves garlic, minced	3
1	bay leaf	1
5	peppercorns	5
3 cups	white wine	750 mL
4 cups	chicken or vegetable stock	1 L
2 cups	heavy cream (35% M.F.)	500 mL

salt and pepper to taste
crème fraîche for garnish
fresh basil for garnish

Steam snow peas until soft and bright green.
Drain, rinse under cold water and reserve.

In a heavy saucepan heat butter over medium
heat until it becomes frothy. Add shallots and
garlic; reduce heat to low; cover and cook
vegetables until translucent, about 8 to 10
minutes. Add bay leaf and peppercorns; raise heat
to medium-high and deglaze pan with wine.

Lower heat to simmer and reduce wine mixture
by half. Add stock; bring to a boil and reduce by
half. Add heavy cream; bring to a boil and reduce
by a quarter. Remove bay leaf and black
peppercorns.

In a blender, puree cream mixture and snow peas
in batches until smooth. Strain through a sieve
and return to saucepan. Adjust seasoning with
salt and pepper and bring to serving
temperature.

Ladle in warmed cream-soup bowls; garnish with
a dollop of crème fraîche and a sprig of fresh
basil.

Serves 4 to 6

FRESH MUSHROOM AND
GREEN ONION SOUP

THE CREEK IN CATHEDRAL BISTRO,
REGINA, SASKATCHEWAN

Choose tender, young green onions or scallions
for this delightful soup. The chef notes that it may
be refrigerated overnight or frozen for future
enjoyment.

3-4	bunches green onion (16-20)	3-4
¾ cup	butter	175 mL
½ tsp	cayenne pepper	2 mL
3 tbsp	all-purpose flour	45 mL
6 cups	chicken stock	1.5 L
1 lb	button mushrooms, sliced	500 g
salt and white pepper to taste		
½ cup	sour cream	125 mL
chopped chives for garnish		

Trim, rinse and coarsely chop green onions,
including the green tops. Melt butter in a large
saucepan over medium heat until foaming; stir in
green onions and cayenne pepper. Reduce heat
to low, cover and cook, stirring occasionally for
10 minutes; be careful not to brown.

Stir in flour and whisk over low heat for about 2
minutes. Gradually add chicken stock; increase
heat to medium and bring to a boil. Reduce heat
to medium-low and simmer uncovered for about
10 minutes, stirring occasionally.

Stir in ¾ of the mushrooms; simmer until soft. In a
blender, puree the soup in batches until smooth
and creamy. Return puree to saucepan, bring to
serving temperature and adjust seasoning with
salt and pepper. Add remaining mushrooms and
cook 1 minute.

Garnish each bowl with a dollop of sour cream
and chopped chives.

Serves 6

CREAM OF CAULIFLOWER SOUP

KINGSBRAE GARDEN CAFÉ,
ST. ANDREWS BY-THE-SEA, NB

Ellen Tremblay's smooth and creamy soup is an ideal starter for a special dinner. We prepared this soup twice, once using heavy cream and the second time using blend (12% M.F.). While the heavy cream created a full-bodied soup, the flavour was not compromised in the lighter version.

¼ cup	butter	50 mL
1	medium onion, chopped	1
2-3	cloves garlic, minced	2-3
1	large cauliflower	1
1	large potato, peeled and cubed	1
3 cups	chicken stock	750 mL
1 cup	heavy cream (35% M.F.)	250 mL

salt and pepper to taste
grated aged cheddar cheese as garnish
parsley sprigs as garnish

Melt butter in a large stockpot over low heat. Stir in onion and garlic; cover and cook on low, stirring often, until translucent but not browned, about 15 minutes.

Wash and divide cauliflower into florets. Add cauliflower and potato and stir to coat; turn up heat and sauté 15 minutes. Stir in stock and bring to a boil; reduce to simmer and cook, covered, until vegetables are tender.

In a blender, puree in batches and return to pot; stir in cream. Return to serving temperature and adjust seasoning with salt and pepper. Garnish soup with cheese and parsley.

Serves 4 to 6

Roasted Eggplant and Garlic Soup

Vegetarian Soups

We note a new appreciation by chefs to accommodate the health-conscious lifestyle of their patrons. While many soups in this book can be considered vegetarian by replacing chicken or fish stock with vegetable stock or water, we also offer a selection of soups and bisques specifically suggested by our chefs as vegetarian fare.

Be sure to try the creamy Gingered Carrot Soup, a treat from Hatfield Heritage Inn. For heartier fare, sample Black Bean Pumpkin Soup from Willie's Café. Served with crusty bread, this soup is truly a "meal in a bowl."

ROASTED EGGPLANT AND GARLIC SOUP

MURANO, LONDON, ONTARIO

Owner and Executive Chef Bryan Lavery of Murano is an adherent of the "Slow Food" movement; an international group concerned with safeguarding and advancing public awareness of local customs, culinary traditions and agricultural produce, products and livestock, while opposing any harm to the environment. He comments that, "Slow Food is learning to taste again and enjoying a return to the dining table. Most of all it is about enjoying life…slowly."

2	roasted garlic bulbs (recipe follows)	2
2	large eggplants, peeled and cubed	2
1½ cups	chopped onion	375 mL
5 cups	vegetable stock	1.25 L
½ tsp	salt	2 mL
¼ tsp	freshly ground pepper	1 mL
¾ cup	heavy cream (35% M.F.)	175 mL
salt and pepper to taste		
½ cup	finely grated Parmigiano-Reggiano cheese	125 mL

In a large oven proof casserole, combine roasted garlic, eggplant, onion, stock, salt and pepper. Cover and bake in preheated 375°F (190°C) oven for 45 to 60 minutes until vegetables are soft. Uncover, stir and continue to bake an additional 20 to 30 minutes until liquid is slightly reduced and vegetables are roasted.

In a blender, puree soup in batches until smooth and creamy. Return to saucepan and whisk in cream; bring to serving temperature and adjust seasoning with salt and pepper.

Ladle into soup bowls and top with Parmigiano-Reggiano cheese. If desired, place bowls under broiler to melt the cheese.

Serves 6

ROASTED GARLIC

2	whole garlic bulbs	2
2 tsp	olive oil	10 mL
¼ cup	water	50 mL

Rub loose skin from garlic bulbs. Trim root end flat and cut ½-inch (1 cm) from top of each bulb; be careful not to detach individual cloves.

Place bulbs cut side up in a baking dish; drizzle oil over cut ends. Add water to baking dish, cover and bake in preheated 500°F (260°C) oven for 25 to 30 minutes until garlic is soft to the touch. Cool bulbs and squeeze garlic from individual cloves.

Makes ½ cup (125 mL) roasted garlic.

CREAM OF FIDDLEHEAD SOUP

CHANTERELLE COUNTRY INN, NORTH RIVER,
ST. ANN'S BAY, NS

A Maritime delicacy, fiddleheads are harvested
during the late spring or early summer, just before
they unfurl into ferns.

2 cups	fiddleheads	500 mL
2 tbsp	butter	30 mL
3 cups	diced potatoes	750 mL
1 cup	chopped leeks, white part only	250 mL
½ cup	chopped celery	125 mL
1	garlic clove, minced	1
½ cup	diced carrot	125 mL
2 cups	vegetable stock	500 mL
1 cup	heavy cream (35% M.F.)	250 mL
salt and pepper to taste		
grated nutmeg as garnish		

Carefully wash trimmed fiddleheads in several
changes of cold water. Melt butter in a large
stockpot over medium-low heat. Sauté
fiddleheads, potatoes, leeks, celery, garlic and
carrot until tender, stirring frequently.

Remove from burner and cool; puree vegetables
and return to stockpot. Stir in broth and simmer,
covered, for 1 hour.

Stir in cream, reheat; be careful not to boil. Adjust
seasoning with salt and pepper. Serve with a
sprinkling of nutmeg as garnish.

Serves 6 to 8

GINGERED CARROT SOUP

THE HATFIELD HERITAGE INN, HARTLAND, NB

This is an excellent vegetarian soup with a smooth
creamy texture and incredible flavour. Innkeeper
Richard Boulier notes that guests who have never
tried carrot and ginger soup are very surprised
and often request it on return visits.

5 tbsp	butter	75 mL
4 cups	coarsely chopped carrot,	1 L
3 cups	coarsely chopped onion	750 mL
3 tbsp	minced ginger root	45 mL
6 cups	vegetable stock	1.5 L
salt and white pepper to taste		
½ cup	light cream (18% M.F.)	125 mL
chopped parsley for garnish		

Melt butter in a large saucepan over medium-low
heat. Sauté carrot, onion and ginger, stirring
occasionally until vegetables soften, about 10 to
15 minutes. Add stock and bring to a boil.
Reduce heat to simmer; cover loosely and cook
40 minutes.

In a blender, puree soup in batches until smooth
and creamy. Return soup to saucepan; bring back
to simmer and adjust seasoning with salt and
pepper. Add light cream and bring back to
serving temperature.

Serve in warmed soup bowls with a garnish of
fresh chopped parsley.

Serves 6

EGYPTIAN LENTIL SOUP

TEMPEST RESTAURANT, WOLFVILLE, NS

Lentils are an excellent source of protein and a popular staple in Middle Eastern and Indian cuisine. At the Tempest Restaurant, owner and chef Michael Howell finds this red soup a popular choice among his health-conscious patrons.

1½ cups	split red lentils	375 mL
4-6 tbsp	olive oil	60-90 mL
1	large onion, chopped	1
2	large cloves garlic, chopped	2
2 tsp	ground cumin	10 mL
1	medium potato, peeled and cubed	1
2	leeks, white part only, washed and sliced	2
2	beets, peeled and cubed	2
4 cups	vegetable stock	1 L
juice,	1 large lemon	
salt and freshly ground black pepper to taste		
½ cup	chopped flat-leaf parsley	125 mL

Rinse lentils under cold water until water runs clear. In a large pot, heat olive oil over medium heat. Sauté onion and garlic until soft, about 10 minutes. Stir in ground cumin; add potato, leeks, and beets. Sauté over low heat until vegetables start to soften.

Add red lentils, stock and enough water to cover vegetables and bring to a boil. Reduce heat; cover and simmer about 1 hour or until lentils are soft and begin to break down; add additional water if necessary. Skim off foam and discard.

Allow soup to cool 15 minutes. Puree in a blender or food processor until smooth. Stir in lemon juice and adjust seasoning with salt and black pepper. Stir in parsley and bring back to serving temperature.

Serves 6

BLACK BEAN PUMPKIN SOUP

WILLIE'S CAFÉ, LONDON, ONTARIO

Chef Ian Kennard tells us that this soup is a favorite at Willie's Café. This soup is not only tasty, it's also nutritious; it was recently awarded both the Judges and People's Choice categories at the Heart and Stroke Foundation Lunch competition, in London, Ontario.

4 cups	black beans, cooked, drained and rinsed	1 L
1 cup	canned tomatoes, drained and chopped	250 mL
¼ cup	butter	50 mL
1¼ cup	onion, chopped	300 mL
½ cup	shallot, minced	125 mL
4 cloves	garlic, minced	4
4-5 tsp	ground cumin	20-25 mL
1 tsp	salt	5 mL
½ tsp	pepper	2 mL
4 cups	vegetable stock	1 L
2 tbsp	granulated sugar	30 mL
1½ cups	canned pumpkin puree	375 mL
½ cup	dry sherry	125 mL
pinch	each of cinnamon and nutmeg	

salt and pepper to taste
sour cream for garnish

In a food processor, puree beans and tomatoes until smooth; reserve.

Melt butter in a large saucepan over medium heat. Add onion, shallot, garlic, cumin, salt and pepper. Sauté, stirring frequently, until onion is soft and begins to brown, about 10 minutes.

Add bean and tomato puree, stock, sugar, pumpkin, sherry, cinnamon and nutmeg; stir to combine.

Simmer soup, uncovered, stirring occasionally, until soup is thick enough to coat the back of a spoon, about 25 minutes. Adjust seasoning with salt and pepper.

Ladle into warmed soup bowls and garnish with a dollop of sour cream.

Serves 6 to 8

CELERIAC & NEW POTATO BISQUE

HASTINGS HOUSE, SALT SPRING ISLAND, BC

Executive Chef Marcel Kauer has a wealth of delicious creamed soup recipes in his collection. These soups make beautiful first course presentations; their subtle flavours complement and never overpower the entrée course.

In this recipe, Chef Kauer likes to use new potatoes because they have a higher sugar content. If you use older potatoes, it may not be necessary to thicken the soup.

1½ lb	celeriac (celery root), peeled and diced	750 g
¾ lb	new potatoes, peeled and diced	375 g
1	onion, diced	1
2	cloves garlic, minced	2
6 cups	cold water	1.5 L
2 cups	vegetable stock or water	500 mL
2 cups	heavy cream, (35% M.F.)	500 mL
2 tbsp	all-purpose flour, dissolved in 4 tbsp (60 mL) cold water	30 mL

salt and white pepper to taste
Worcestershire and Tabasco sauces to taste
parsley or thyme sprigs as garnish

Combine vegetables, water, stock and cream in a large saucepan. Bring to a boil; reduce heat to a low simmer, cover and cook 45 minutes.

In a blender, puree soup in batches until smooth and creamy. Return to saucepan and bring to a low simmer. If soup needs to be thickened, whisk flour and water together until smooth. Stir into soup, adding only enough to reach desired consistency; simmer 5 minutes.

Adjust seasoning with salt, pepper, Worcestershire and Tabasco sauces. Cover and simmer for an additional 20 minutes.

Ladle into warmed soup bowls and garnish with a sprig of fresh parsley or thyme.

Serves 6 to 8

APPLE & CELERIAC SOUP

THE BRIARS INN AND COUNTRY CLUB,
JACKSON'S POINT, ONTARIO

Executive Chef Trevor Ledlie likes to add a small
amount of red wine vinegar to this soup,
commenting, "It helps bring up the acidity in
order to better reveal the apple flavour."

2 tbsp	butter	30 mL
1	clove garlic, minced	1
½ cup	chopped Spanish onion	125 mL
1 lb	celeriac, peeled and chopped	500 g
2	apples, cored, peeled and chopped	2
1 cup	diced potato	250 mL
6 cups	vegetable stock	1.5 L
½ cup	heavy cream (35% M.F.)	125 mL
1 tsp	red wine vinegar or to taste	5 mL
salt and white pepper to taste		

Melt butter in a large saucepan over medium-low
heat. Sauté garlic and onion, stirring frequently
until soft, about 5 minutes. Add celeriac, apple
and potato; sauté 5 minutes. Add stock and bring
to a boil; reduce heat, cover and simmer for 45
minutes.

In a blender, puree soup in batches until smooth
and creamy. Return soup to saucepan; stir in
heavy cream and bring to serving temperature.

Adjust seasoning with red wine vinegar, adding a
little at a time to obtain desired flavour. Add salt
and white pepper to taste.

Ladle in warmed soup bowls.

Serves 6

CAULIFLOWER AND RED PEPPER SOUP

SMITH AND LATHAM, ST. MARYS, ONTARIO

Prepare this soup when cauliflowers and red peppers are newly harvested. At Smith and Latham, Chef Robert Smith garnishes his soup with chopped chives, sautéed leeks or Stilton cheese.

½ cup	unsalted butter	125 mL
1	large red bell pepper, seeded and finely chopped	1
1	large sweet onion, peeled and finely chopped	1
1	large cauliflower, separated into florets and chopped	1
1	large clove garlic, mashed	1
2 cups	water	500 mL
salt and pepper to taste		
2 oz	Stilton cheese, crumbled	60 g

Melt butter in a large saucepan. Add pepper, onion, cauliflower and garlic; cook over medium-low heat, stirring often, until vegetables have softened, about 12 minutes. Cover vegetables with 2 cups water and bring to a boil. Reduce heat, cover and simmer until vegetables are soft, about 20 minutes.

Puree soup in a blender; adjust seasoning with salt and pepper.

Serve garnished with crumbled Stilton cheese.

Serves 4

French Onion & Cépe Soup with Oka Cheese Croutes

Hearty Soups

Hearty soups, like casseroles and stews, make excellent one-dish meals, especially when accompanied by bread and salad. In this section, you will find traditional fare such as French Onion and Cèpe Mushroom Soup from Chives Canadian Bistro and Quick Romano Bean and Pasta Soup from the Italian Gourmet, Halifax.

This section also features unusual recipes that use exotic ingredients. Be sure to sample Posole Soup, an intriguing Mexican-style dish from Chef Michael Howell of Tempest Restaurant, or Thai Coconut and Mussel Soup from Solé Restaurant and Wine Bar.

FRENCH ONION & CÈPE SOUP WITH OKA CHEESE CROUTES

CHIVES CANADIAN BISTRO, HALIFAX, NS

Chef Craig Flinn has created a very different onion soup with this recipe and it's a winner. Unlike traditional French onion soup, this version is made with chicken or vegetable stock instead of beef stock, and incorporates dried cèpe (porcini) mushrooms plumped with vermouth and balsamic vinegar.

2 oz	dehydrated cèpe mushrooms, chopped	60 g
¾ cup	dry, white Vermouth	175 mL
3 tbsp	white balsamic vinegar	45 mL
3 tbsp	unsalted butter	45 mL
1	shallot, thinly sliced	1
3	cloves garlic, minced	3
2 lb	onion, peeled & thinly sliced (red, Spanish & sweet onion combination)	1 kg
1 tsp	brown sugar	5 mL
4 sprigs	fresh thyme (1tsp/5 mL dried)	4
4-5 cups	chicken or vegetable stock	1-1.25 L
¼ tsp	ground cumin	1 mL
salt and pepper to taste		
6-8	seasoned croutes (page 94)	6-8
1 cup	grated Oka cheese (optional: Port Salut)	250 mL

In a medium bowl, combine mushrooms, Vermouth and balsamic vinegar. Cover and allow mushrooms to re-hydrate, about 30 minutes. With a slotted spoon, remove mushrooms and reserve. Pass mushroom liquid through a fine mesh sieve to remove any grit and return liquid to mushrooms.

In a large, heavy-based saucepan, heat butter over medium-high heat. Add shallots, garlic and onions; sauté, stirring frequently, until onions begin to take colour, about 10 minutes. Add brown sugar to onions and stir to combine. Cover saucepan, reduce heat to low and continue cooking, stirring occasionally until onions caramelize, about 45 minutes.

Return heat to medium-high; add re-hydrated mushroom mixture and thyme; stir and cook 2 minutes. Add stock; reduce heat to simmer and cook 30 minutes. Adjust seasoning with ground cumin and salt and pepper to taste.

Pour hot soup into ovenproof soup bowls. Place a croute on top and cover with Oka cheese. Set bowls under broiler and heat until cheese lightly browns.

Serves 6 to 8

THAI COCONUT & MUSSEL SOUP

SOLÉ RESTAURANT & WINE BAR, WATERLOO, ONTARIO

The heat intensity of this soup depends on the amount of curry paste and chilies used. The chef comments, "While creams, butter and other dairy products are never used in authentic Thai cooking; if you find the soup too spicy, you can add a little heavy cream as you adjust the seasoning."

½ tsp	black peppercorns	2 mL
1 tsp	fennel seed	5 mL
1 tsp	cumin seed	5 mL
1 tsp	coriander seed	5 mL
2 tsp	vegetable oil	10 mL
½	large red onion, chopped	½
¾ cup	white wine	175 mL
¾ cup	water	175 mL
1 stalk	lemon grass, white part only, peeled and sliced	1
5	Kaffir lime leaves* (optional, 2 tsp/10 mL lime zest)	5
2½ lb	fresh mussels	1.25 kg
2 tsp	vegetable oil (2ⁿᵈ amount)	10 mL
½	large white onion, chopped	½
2	cloves garlic, minced	2
1½ -inch	piece ginger root, peeled and grated	3.5 cm
1-2	red Thai chilies, seeded, finely diced	1-2
1-3 tsp	mild red curry paste	5-15 mL
3 cans	coconut milk (14 oz/420 g)	3
1	large bunch cilantro, chopped	1
3-4 tbsp	fresh lime juice	45-60 mL

salt to taste

cilantro sprigs for garnish

In a skillet, toast peppercorns, fennel, cumin and coriander seeds over medium-high heat, shaking frequently, until fragrant, about 3 minutes. Finely crush spices with a mortar and pestle and reserve.

Heat oil in a large saucepan over medium heat. Add red onion and sauté until softened. Add wine, water, lemon grass and lime leaves to saucepan; bring to a boil. Scrub mussels, discarding any that don't open when lightly tapped. Add to saucepan. Cover and steam mussels until fully opened, about 5 to 7 minutes; discard any that do not open. Remove 80% of mussels; reserve and refrigerate mussel meat and discard shells.

Continue to simmer cooking liquid and remaining mussels for an additional 10 minutes. Strain cooking liquid through a fine mesh strainer and reserve liquid; discard pulp and shells.

In a clean saucepan, heat second amount of vegetable oil over medium heat. Add white onion, garlic, ginger root, chili pepper and curry paste; sauté until onion is softened. Add reserved cooking liquid, coconut milk, toasted spices and cilantro. Bring to a boil; reduce heat to simmer, cover lightly and cook 30 minutes, stirring occasionally.

In a blender, puree soup in batches until smooth. Return soup to saucepan and adjust seasoning with lime juice and salt to taste. Add reserved mussels and bring to serving temperature.

Garnish with sprigs of fresh cilantro.

Serves 4 to 6

* Kaffir lime leaves, similar in appearance to the bay leaf, come from the kaffir lime tree, native to Southeast Asia. You can find them in Asian markets, generally in dried form, but occasionally fresh, which have a more intense fragrance.

POSOLE SOUP

TEMPEST RESTAURANT, WOLFVILLE, NS

Chef Michael Howell comments, "This Mexican soup is a great change from traditional chicken soup and is very easy to prepare." Canned hominy (posole) and poblano chilies are available in the international food section of most large supermarkets.

This recipe makes a large quantity, but don't worry as it freezes well, in the unlikely event that you have leftovers.

3-4 lb	chicken, cut in pieces	1.5 -2 kg
2 qt	water	2 L
2 tsp	vegetable oil	10 mL
2	carrots, peeled and chopped	2
1	large onion, chopped	1
3	stalks celery, chopped	3
4	cloves garlic, minced	4
1 tsp	grated ginger root	5 mL
1 lb	yucca, peeled and chopped	500 g
1 can	hominy, drained (19 oz/570 g)	1
1 can	poblano chili peppers, drained, seeded and chopped (19 oz/570 g)	1
1	chicken bouillon cube	1
3 tbsp	cornstarch, dissolved in 3 tbsp (45 mL) water	45 mL
½ cup	fresh lime juice	125 mL
salt and pepper to taste		
½ cup	chopped cilantro	125 mL

In a large stockpot, combine chicken pieces, water, carrot, onion, celery, garlic, ginger root and yucca. Bring to a boil; reduce heat to simmer, cover and cook 25 minutes or until chicken is cooked.

Remove chicken from liquid; reserve and when chicken is cool enough to handle, remove and shred meat.

Add hominy, chili peppers, shredded chicken and bouillon cube to stockpot. Bring to a simmer and cook for 5 minutes. Add cornstarch mixture and cook for 2 minutes to thicken. Adjust seasoning with lime juice, salt, pepper and 1/4 cup cilantro.

Ladle into warmed soup bowls and garnish with remaining chopped cilantro.

Serves 8 to 10

QUICK ROMANO BEAN AND PASTA SOUP

THE ITALIAN GOURMET, HALIFAX, NS

Chef and owner Kate Abato suggests cooking the pasta separately so that it does not absorb the liquid from the soup. At the Italian Gourmet, she serves this hearty soup in many variations, at times using red or green peppers, squash or potato as the vegetable combination or substituting red kidney or white cannellini beans. You may use either vegetable or beef stock for a different flavoured soup.

1½ cups	chopped mixed vegetables (onion, leek, carrot, celery)	375 mL
2	cloves garlic, minced	2
4 tbsp	olive oil	60 mL
1-28 oz	can Italian plum tomatoes, coarsely chopped	796 mL
4 cups	chicken stock	1 L
1 tbsp	each chopped fresh basil, oregano and parsley (1 tsp /5mL each dried)	15 mL
pinch	red pepper flakes	
2 cups	cooked Romano beans	500 mL
½ cup	Italian soup pasta such as stellete, farfaline, ditali or filini, cooked al dente	125 mL
salt and freshly ground black pepper to taste		
½ cup	freshly grated Parmesan cheese as garnish	125 mL

Sauté vegetables and garlic in olive oil over medium heat until onions are translucent, about 10 minutes. Stir in tomatoes, stock, herbs, red pepper flakes; simmer 15 minutes, stirring occasionally. Add Romano beans and simmer 10 minutes, stirring occasionally. Continue to cook until vegetables are tender. Adjust seasoning with salt and pepper.

In a separate pot, cook pasta according to package directions. Drain; do not rinse.

To serve, place 3 tablespoons of cooked pasta in each soup bowl and top with soup. Serve garnished with grated Parmesan cheese and crusty bread.

Serves 6

PHEASANT & WILD RICE SOUP

Pheasant and prairie wild rice make this soup truly Canadian. A hearty soup with a slight wild-game flavour, it serves well as a main course accompanied with hot bread and Canadian cheddar cheese.

   You may substitute chicken if pheasant is not available; this will create a milder flavoured soup.

2 cups	cooked wild rice*	500 mL
½ cup	butter	125 mL
1	medium onion, finely chopped	1
2	carrots, peeled and diced	2
3	stalks celery, diced	3
5 tbsp	all-purpose flour	75 mL
5 cups	chicken stock	1.25 L
2 cups	blend (12% M.F.)	500 mL
2 cups	diced, cooked pheasant, (optional: chicken)	500 mL
1 tsp	rosemary, minced, (½ tsp/2 mL dried)	5 mL
salt and pepper to taste		

Prepare rice according to directions and reserve.

In a large saucepan, melt butter over medium heat. Sauté onion, carrot and celery; stir frequently until soft but not browned, about 10 minutes. Stir in flour and cook for 1 minute. Stirring constantly, gradually add stock; bring to a boil and cook for 2 minutes.

Add blend, pheasant, rosemary and rice; reduce heat to low and gently cook for 30 minutes; be careful not to boil. Adjust seasoning with salt and pepper.

Serve in warmed soup bowls.

Serves 6 to 8

* Wild Rice Quick-Soak Method: In a fine mesh sieve, rinse 1 cup (250 mL) wild rice with cold water. In a saucepan, bring 3 cups water to a boil. Stir rice into boiling water; return to a boil and cook 5 minutes. Remove from heat and reserve, covered for 1 hour. Drain and reserve rice. Makes 2 cups cooked rice.

CREAMY GARLIC SOUP WITH BLACKENED TIGER SHRIMP

THE WINDSOR HOUSE OF ST. ANDREWS,
ST. ANDREWS-BY-THE-SEA, NB

Chef Peter Woodworth notes that this soup is for garlic lovers. The amount of garlic you use depends upon your personal taste.

8-12	medium to large garlic cloves, peeled and minced	8 -12
1	small Spanish onion, chopped	1
2 tbsp	olive oil	30 mL
⅔ cup	white wine	150 mL
2	fresh sage leaves	2
1 tbsp	fresh thyme leaves	15 mL
1	large potato, peeled and diced	1
4 cups	chicken stock	1 L
½ cup	heavy cream (35% M.F.)	125 mL
salt and pepper to taste		
12	raw tiger shrimps, peeled and deveined	12
2 tbsp	Cajun seasoning	30 mL
2 tbsp	olive oil	30 mL

In a heavy-bottomed pot, sauté onion and garlic in 2 tablespoons olive oil over medium heat until translucent. Deglaze with white wine. Stir in herbs, stock, potatoes; season with salt and pepper. Bring to a boil; add cream and return to a boil immediately. Lower heat to medium-low and simmer 10 to 15 minutes, until potatoes are softened.

In blender, puree soup in batches. Return to pot and keep warm.

Rinse and pat dry shrimp; toss in Cajun spice. Heat olive oil in a skillet over high heat; sauté shrimp until just cooked.

Pour soup into individual bowls and top with shrimp.

Serves 4 to 6

FAMED PICKLE SOUP

SANDWICH PATCH CAFÉ, NORTH BATTLEFORD, SASKATCHEWAN

This is one of the most unusual soups in this collection. We admit our earlier skepticism about dill pickle juice as an ingredient but the soup's flavour is subtle, unique and very, very good. We can see why it is a menu favorite at the Sandwich Patch Café.

3 tbsp	butter	45 mL
1 cup	diced onion	250 mL
½ cup	diced celery	125 mL
½ cup	diced carrot	125 mL
2½ cups	chicken stock	625 mL
2½ cups	homogenized milk (3.5% M.F.)	625 mL
1 cup	diced potato	250 mL
¼ cup	all-purpose flour	50 mL
⅔ cup	dill pickle juice	150 mL
1 cup	heavy cream (35% M.F.)	250 mL
⅔ cup	diced dill pickle	150 mL
4 tbsp	chopped fresh dill	60 mL
salt and pepper to taste		
sprigs of fresh dill for garnish		

Melt butter in a large saucepan over medium heat. Add onion, celery and carrot; sauté until onion is softened, about 6 minutes. Add potato, chicken stock and milk; cook, being careful not to boil, until vegetables are tender.

In a bowl, whisk flour and ½ cup (125 mL) of the liquid from the saucepan until smooth. Carefully add the flour mixture to the soup; stir to combine. Add pickle juice, cream, diced pickles and chopped dill to the soup and continue to heat, without boiling. Adjust seasoning with salt and pepper.

Serve in heated bowls with a small sprig of fresh dill.

Serves 6 to 8

WILD MUSHROOM SOUP

RESTAURANT LES FOUGÈRES, CHELSEA, QUÉBEC

You can almost taste the woodland earthiness of the Gatineau Hills when you dip your spoon into this delicious soup from Chef and Proprietor Charles Part of Restaurant Les Fougères. This soup, with its delicate balance of mature flavours, is a perfect choice for chilly autumn or cold winter meals.

1½ cups	dried wild mushrooms, (morel, porcini, etc.)	375 mL
2 cups	warm water	500 mL
2 tbsp	butter	30 mL
1	onion, finely chopped	1
2	cloves garlic, minced	2
1 cup	sliced portabella mushrooms,	250 mL
2 tbsp	all-purpose flour	30 mL
½ cup	dry sherry	125 mL
3 cups	chicken stock	750 mL
½ cup	heavy cream (35% M.F.)	125 mL
1 tbsp	chopped fresh tarragon, (1tsp/5 mL dried)	15 mL

salt and pepper to taste
lemon zest for garnish

In a bowl, soak dried mushrooms in warm water for 30 minutes. Remove mushrooms with a slotted spoon and reserve. Pass soaking liquid through a fine mesh sieve to remove any sand and grit; reserve liquid.

Melt butter in a large saucepan over medium-low heat. Cover and cook onion and garlic until softened, stirring frequently. Add portobella mushrooms, wild mushrooms and flour; stir to combine and cook for 2 minutes, stirring constantly.

Add sherry, chicken stock and reserved mushroom liquid; bring to a boil. Add cream and tarragon; reduce heat to simmer and cook 20 minutes until slightly thickened. Adjust seasoning with salt and pepper to taste.

Ladle soup into warmed soup bowls and garnish with lemon zest.

Serves 6

SMOKED GOUDA CHEESE SOUP

THE MAHLE HOUSE RESTAURANT, NANAIMO, BC

Chef Maureen Louck's rich, smokey cheese soup will warm you on a chilly day.

Be sure to use genuine Dutch Gouda cheese when making this soup. North American, Gouda-style cheese is available but is frequently not aged and is very mild in flavour.

¼ cup	butter	50 mL
1	large onion, chopped	1
2 tsp	minced garlic	10 mL
1 tbsp	all-purpose flour	15 mL
6 cups	chicken stock	1.5 L
salt and white pepper to taste		
2 cups	heavy cream (35% M.F.)	500 mL
8 oz	smoked Gouda cheese, grated	250 g
chopped fresh chives or basil for garnish		
	(optional: green onion, thinly sliced)	

In a large, heavy-bottomed saucepan, melt butter over medium-low heat. Add onion; cover and cook until soft but not browned, about 10 minutes. Add garlic and cook, stirring often, for 2 minutes. Whisk in flour and stir constantly, for 1 minute. Stir in chicken stock; season with salt and white pepper to taste; bring to a boil.

Reduce heat to a low simmer, partly cover and cook, stirring frequently, for 30 to 45 minutes.

Stir in heavy cream and cook, stirring frequently, until slightly reduced. Add cheese, stir until melted and smooth.

In a blender, puree soup in batches until smooth and creamy. Strain if necessary and return to saucepan; reheat gently.

Ladle into bowls and garnish with chives or basil.

Serves 6

MINESTRONE SOUP

SIRENELLA RISTORANTE, CHARLOTTETOWN, PEI

Chef and owner Italo Marzari suggests adding a ham bone to the cooking broth to enrich the flavour of this soup. Should you wish to freeze the soup, add the pasta just at serving time.

2 tbsp	vegetable oil	30 mL
1 cup	diced onion	250 mL
2	garlic cloves, crushed	2
5 cups	chicken stock	1.25 L
2	carrots, peeled and diced	2
1½ cups	diced red or green sweet pepper	375 mL
2	small zucchini, seeded and diced	2
1½ cups	small pasta	375 mL
28 oz	can Italian-style tomatoes, chopped	796 mL
2 cups	diced cooked ham	500 mL
14 oz	can chickpeas, drained and rinsed	398 mL
14 oz	can red kidney beans, drained and rinsed	398 mL
4 oz	fresh spinach	125 g
1 tsp	dried thyme	5 mL
¾ tsp	dried savory	3 mL
¾ tsp	dried basil or oregano	3 mL
salt and pepper to taste		

Heat oil in a large saucepan over medium heat. Sauté onion until tender, about 4 minutes. Add garlic, chicken stock, carrots, sweet peppers and zucchini; bring to a boil. Reduce heat and simmer vegetables until tender.

Add pasta, diced tomatoes, ham, chickpeas, kidney beans, spinach and herbs; simmer 10 minutes or until pasta is al dente. Adjust seasoning with pepper and salt.

Serves 6 to 8

ROASTED TOMATO AND EGGPLANT SOUP WITH CUCUMBER RAITA

ON THE TWENTY RESTAURANT AND WINE BAR, JORDAN, ONTARIO

Chef Rob Fracchioni shares what he calls a "simple soup – easy enough for an average home cook to create and one that has no crazy ingredients and is not difficult to prepare." You will not be disappointed with his choice.

2 lb	eggplant	1 kg
½ lb	vine-ripened tomatoes	250 g
Extra virgin olive oil		
2 tbsp	butter	30 mL
1	small red onion, chopped	1
1	stalk celery, chopped	1
1	small carrot, chopped	1
5 cups	chicken stock	1.25 L
2	cloves garlic, minced	2
1½ tsp	fennel seed	7 mL
1 cup	heavy cream (35% M.F.)	250 mL
salt and pepper to taste		
Cucumber Raita (recipe follows)		

Brush eggplant and tomatoes with olive oil. Prick eggplant with a fork, cut in half lengthwise and arrange cut side down on a baking sheet with the tomatoes. Bake in a preheated 375°F (190°C) oven for 35 to 40 minutes, until eggplant is cooked. Cool vegetables slightly; remove skin, chop pulp and reserve.

Heat butter in a saucepan over medium heat. Sauté onion, celery and carrot until tender, about 10 minutes. Add roasted vegetables, chicken stock, garlic and fennel seed; bring to a boil. Reduce heat, cover and simmer for 45 minutes.

In a blender, puree soup in batches until smooth. Bring soup back to a simmer; whisk in cream and adjust seasoning with salt and pepper.

Serve in warmed soup bowls with a spoonful of Cucumber Raita.

Serves 6

CUCUMBER RAITA

Yogurt salads are common to Indian cuisine and offer a cooling taste contrast with spicy dishes.

1 cup	peeled seeded and finely diced cucumber	250 mL
1	small clove garlic, minced	1
½ tsp	ground cumin	2 mL
1 tbsp	chopped cilantro	15 mL
½ cup	plain, whole milk yogurt	125 mL
salt and cayenne pepper to taste		

Blot excess cucumber moisture with paper towels. In a bowl, whisk cucumber, garlic, cumin, cilantro and yogurt until combined. Adjust seasoning with salt and pepper.

Refrigerate at least 1 hour for flavours to combine.

Makes 1¼ cups (300 mL) raita

RED ONION AND CHORIZO SAUSAGE SOUP

GARDENS' CAFÉ AT ROYAL BOTANICAL GARDENS, HAMILTON, ONTARIO

Executive Chef Steven Soloduk of Compton and Greenland Fine Foods and Catering, food purveyors to the Gardens' Café at Royal Botanical Gardens, shares with us his uniquely flavoured red onion soup.

We advise using a very heavy or cast iron stockpot to make this soup, as the oil and onions are cooked at a very high temperature for a considerable amount of time.

3	chorizo sausages	3
½ cup	vegetable oil	125 mL
12 cups	thinly sliced red onion	3 L
1 tsp	salt	5 mL
½ tsp	pepper	2 mL
2½ tsp	dried thyme	12 mL
6 cups	water	1.5 L

Arrange sausages on a foil-lined baking sheet. Prick casings with a fork to release excess fat. Bake in a preheated 350°F (180°C) oven until cooked, about 20 to 25 minutes. Cool; slice into rounds and reserve.

Heat heavy-bottomed stockpot over high heat for 1 minute. Carefully add oil and heat for 30 seconds. Add onion; quickly and thoroughly stir in the oil. Keep the heat on high and cook onion for 3 to 4 minutes, stirring frequently. Season with salt, pepper and thyme. Continue to stir and cook until onions begin to caramelize, about 6 to 8 minutes.

Reduce heat to low; cover and cook 30 minutes, stirring occasionally.

Stir water into onion mixture and bring to a boil. Add sausage rounds; reduce heat to simmer and cook 15 minutes. If sausages release excess fat, skim it from surface of soup and discard. Adjust seasoning, and serve.

Serves 6

Stocks & Garnishes

Your friends and family deserve the best. That's why it's worth taking the time to prepare homemade stocks for your soup, chowder or bisque. Use the freshest ingredients, skim off the surface fat and impurities, and be sure to simmer the stock until it reduces somewhat to ensure a rich, flavourful soup.

When you're ready to serve your soup, chowder or bisque take a few extra seconds with the final presentation. Serve hot soups in warm bowls, choose unusual dishware, and garnish using fresh herbs, swirls of flavoured oil, cream, pesto or a dollop of sour cream.

BASIC CHICKEN STOCK

PRAIRIE ORCHARD TEA HOUSE,
NEEPAWA, MANITOBA

It is the opinion of Chef Mary Anne Nylen at Prairie Orchard that soup, like everything else in life, needs a good base to achieve perfection, and the best base for soup is homemade stock.

	Rack from 3 large roasted chickens or 3 lbs chicken thighs and legs, roasted	
1	large onion, chopped	1
1	large potato, peeled and chopped	1
2	medium carrots, chopped	2
2	stalks celery, chopped	2
2-3	bay leaves	2-3
10	peppercorns	10
2½-3	quarts filtered water	2.5 L-3 L

Place all ingredients in a large stockpot. Chicken should be completely covered with water. Slowly bring to a boil, skimming often. Reduce heat to simmer and cook uncovered, 5 to 6 hours, skimming occasionally; add water to cover bones if necessary. Cool, then strain out all the solids.

Makes 8 to 10 cups (2 to 2.5 L)

FISH STOCK

Use lean, white-fleshed fish such as cod, haddock, halibut, pollock or ocean perch to make fish stock. Fish with a high fat content will have a strong flavour that is not suited for delicate stock.

2½ lbs	fish trimmings with some flesh attached (skeletons, heads)	1.25 kg
5 cups	filtered cold water	1.25 L
1 cup	dry white wine	250 mL
1	carrot, peeled and chopped	1
1	small onion, peeled and chopped	1
10	fresh sprigs of parsley	10
2-3	sprigs of fresh thyme (pinch of dried thyme)	2-3
1	bay leaf	1

Discard tail, fat, gills, skin and all traces of blood from fish trimmings. Rinse with cold water and place fish in a stockpot. Add water to almost cover the bones, plus wine to completely cover. Add remaining ingredients and stir to combine.

Cook over medium heat until the liquid begins to boil; adjust temperature to maintain a simmer and cook uncovered, for 20 to 30 minutes. With a wooden spoon, occasionally stir and press the bones to release more flavour.

Remove from heat; strain ingredients through a fine mesh strainer lined with cheesecloth. With a spoon, skim the surface to remove any fat. Refrigerate for up to 3 days or freeze up to 2 months.

Makes 5 cups (1.25 L) stock

ROASTED VEGETABLE STOCK

Prepare this stock when summer vegetables are at their freshest and store in containers in the freezer for future use.

2	medium carrots, peeled & chopped	2
3	small onions, chopped	3
2	stalks celery, chopped	2
3	leeks, white part only, chopped	3
1	medium fennel bulb, chopped	1
1	large tomato, chopped	1
2 tbsp	olive oil	30 mL
12 cups	cold filtered water	3 l
½ bunch	green onions, chopped	½
5 sprigs	Italian parsley	5

Preheat oven to 325°F (160°C). Place carrots, onions, leeks, fennel and tomato in a large roasting pan. Drizzle with olive oil; toss vegetables to coat. Roast 45 minutes or until vegetables are tender and begin to colour.

Transfer to a large stockpot and cover with cold water. Add green onions and parsley sprigs; bring to a boil. Skim any foam that appears on top; reduce heat to simmer and cook uncovered, for 2 hours.

Strain and refrigerate or freeze for future use.

Makes 8 to 10 cups (2 to 2.5 L)

CRÈME FRAÎCHE

Commonly used in French cooking, crème fraîche is a thickened, smooth cream with a slight acrid, nutty flavour. In France, the utilization of unpasteurized cream is common, but in North America we must use pasteurized cream which lacks the bacteria needed for thickening. Traditional crème fraîche is sold in some specialty markets but is also easy to duplicate at home.

1 cup	heavy cream (35% M.F.)	250 mL
2 tbsp	buttermilk	30 mL

In a glass bowl, combine cream and buttermilk. Cover and let stand at room temperature for 8 to 24 hours or until thickened. Stir and refrigerate for up to 10 days.

Makes 1 cup (250 mL)

SKILLET CROUTONS

These basic croutons adapt well to seasoning. Before removing from skillet, sprinkle with your favorite herb or spice and stir a couple of times.

3 tbsp	butter	45 mL
3 slices	good-quality white bread, crusts removed, cut into large cubes	3

In a skillet, heat butter over medium-high heat. Add croutons and stir until brown and crispy.

SEASONED BUTTER CROUTES

Tasty croutes are ideal accompaniments to onion and other soups. Serve them as a topping or on the side, at room temperature or crisped for a few minutes in a 350°F (180°C) oven.

6 tbsp	butter	90 mL
Choice of seasonings, (choose 1 of the following)		
	2 tbsp finely chopped chives	30 mL
OR		
	3 oil-packed, sun-dried tomatoes, patted dry and chopped	3
OR		
	2 tbsp grated Parmigiano-Reggiano cheese	30 mL
OR		
1-2	garlic cloves, minced	1-2
small sourdough or French baguette cut in ½-inch (2.5 cm) diagonal slices		
freshly ground pepper		

Combine butter and your choice of seasoning in a food processor. Pulse until well combined; remove to a small bowl and reserve.

Arrange bread slices on a baking sheet and bake in preheated 350°F (180°C) oven until lightly toasted on one side, about 2 minutes. Remove from oven. Turn slices over; spread with seasoned butter and sprinkle with freshly ground pepper.

Return to oven and bake until bread is dry and tops are lightly browned, about 6 to 10 minutes.

Cool completely and store in an airtight container.

INDEX

MORE ADVENTURES OF THE SUPERKIDS
LIBRARY

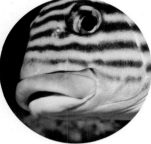

Animal Noses

Written by Elizabeth Chobanian

ROWLAND READING FOUNDATION

MIDDLETON, WISCONSIN

What if you had a different nose?

No, not a nose like *that*.

An *animal* nose!

Animal noses can be many shapes and sizes.

Some are big.

ELEPHANT SEAL

Some are little.

RABBIT

2

Some look like
what you'd
think a nose
would look like.

TIGER

Some look like
nothing you've ever
seen before.

MANDRILL

3

The shape of an animal's nose helps tell you how the animal uses it.

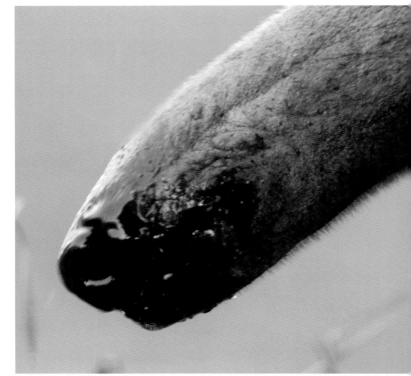

A stubby nose may help an animal dig for its dinner.

PIG

A long nose can be perfect for sticking into anthills. A long tongue can be perfect for gobbling up ants.

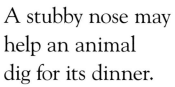

ANTEATER

4

This is a nose!
Really!

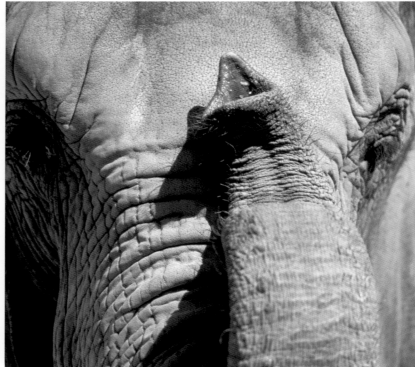

A nose like this can
help an animal
make its way
along a dim tunnel.

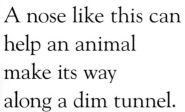

STAR-NOSED MOLE

An animal may
even use its nose
to scratch an itch
and take a bath!

ELEPHANT

5

Many animals use their nose to breathe and smell, as people do.

This is a nostril.

The holes in a nose are "nostrils." This robin has nostrils in its bill.

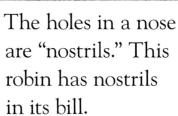

ROBIN

Some animals can close their nostrils to keep sand out of their nose.

CAMEL

6

Other animals can close
their nostrils
when it's time
for a swim.

SEAL

A skunk can't close its nostrils.
Too bad for it!

SKUNK

But these animals are different.

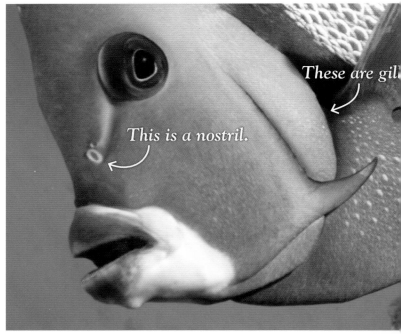

This is a nostril.

These are gill

A snake breathes
with its nose
but uses its
tongue to smell.

SNAKE

A fish smells with
its nostrils but
breathes with
its gills.

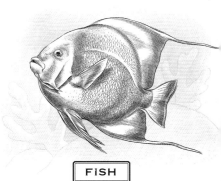

FISH

Here's a different spot for a nostril!

This big whale breathes with just one nostril. It cannot smell much of anything.

WHALE

Insects don't really have noses. Insects tend to smell with their antennas and breathe with holes in their sides.

BUTTERFLY

Many animals can smell things that people can't. Those smells tell animals a lot.

A hunting animal can smell a deer from a long way away.

WOLF

But deer smell well, too. A deer sniffs the air a lot. If it smells something scary, it takes off—fast!

DEER

10

This animal can't see well.
It finds its way
with its nose.

BADGER

This animal can find the
same pond where it
first hatched. How?
Perhaps by smelling.

SALAMANDER

Before a bison picks a
mate, he first checks
out how she smells.

BISON

How can a mama bat
find her baby?
By its smell.

BAT

Many animals will pee and poop here and there to leave their smell for other animals. The smell says, *This home is mine!*

RHINO

When a cat rubs itself on your leg, it is leaving a smell that says, *This kid is mine!*

CAT

13

Dogs have some of the best noses.

A person reads a newspaper to get the news. A dog "reads" smells.

That's why dogs sniff one another all the time.

What did you eat today?

Where have you been?

How do you feel?

Your smell will tell me.

You are not a dog. You are not a camel or a snake. You are a kid.
That's O.K. Your nose is still very useful.

Your nose lets you breathe.

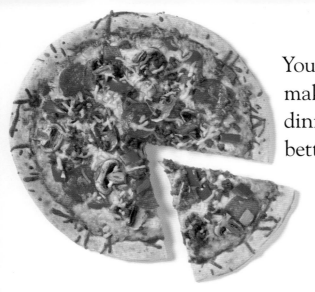

Your nose makes your dinner taste better.

Your nose tells you if things are fresh.

It also tells you if something stinks.

You can perch your glasses on your nose.

You can even
rub noses
with someone
you love.